Baseball Umpires Guidebook
Volume I — Proper Positioning

From the Publishers of *Referee* Magazine
and the National Association of Sports Officials

BASEBALL UMPIRES' GUIDEBOOK
Volume I — Proper Positioning

Original work by Mark R. Ambrosius

Edited by Scott Ehret and Bill Topp, Editor, *Referee* Magazine

Graphics and layout by Matt Bowen

Copyright © 1993 by Referee Enterprises, Inc., P.O. Box 161, Franksville, Wis. 53126

Third printing © 2000

Printed in the United States of America

Table of Contents

page 7 .... **Acknowledgments**
9 .... **Introduction**
11 .... **Philosophy of Positioning**
11 .... **Theory of Proper Positioning**
12 .... **Mechanics of Positioning**
12 ....The Plate Umpire
12 .... Inside-protector work
12 .... Outside-protector work
13 .... Practicing your stance
13 .... Focusing on the pitch
13 .... Here comes the pitch
13 .... Making adjustments
16 ....The Base Umpire
16 .... No runners on base
16 .... Runner at first base
16 .... Runners at first and second, second, or third
16 .... Runners at first and third, second and third, bases loaded
16 .... Step up, turn and face the ball
17 .... **Definition of Terms**
20 .... **Case Studies**
21 .... **Bases empty**
22 .... 1. Routine fly ball to right field
24 .... 2. Routine fly ball to left field
26 .... 3. "Trouble" ball to right field
28 .... 4. "Trouble" ball to left field
30 .... 5. Ground ball to the left side
32 .... 6. Ground ball to the right side
34 .... 7. Clean hit to the outfield
36 .... 8. Hit to the outfield, possible extra bases
38 .... 9. Bunt or bouncing ball fielded in "the box"
40 .... Review
41 .... **Runner at first base**
42 .... 10. Pickoff throw to first
44 .... 11. Second-base steal
46 .... 12. Routine fly ball in the "V"
48 .... 13. Routine fly ball down the left-field line
50 .... 14. Routine fly ball down the right-field line
52 .... 15. "Trouble" ball in the "V"
54 .... 16. "Trouble" ball down the left-field line
56 .... 17. "Trouble" ball down the right-field line
58 .... 18. Ground ball to the infield
60 .... 19. Ground ball to the first baseman
62 .... 20. Base hit to left field
64 .... 21. Base hit to right field
66 .... 22. Bunt
68 .... Review
69 .... **Runners at first and second**
   (See also cases 16, 17, 50, 51)
70 .... 23. Pickoff throw to second
72 .... 24. Pickoff throw to first
74 .... 25. Third-base steal

76 .... 26. Routine fly ball in the "V"
78 .... 27. "Trouble" ball in the "V"
80 .... 28. Infield fly
82 .... 29. Ground ball to base umpire's right
84 .... 30. Ground ball to base umpire's left
86 .... 31. Ground ball in the hole between short and third
88 .... 32. Base hit to the outfield
90 .... 33. Bunt
92 .... Review
93 .... **Bases loaded**
   (See also cases 23, 28, 41, 42, 44, 60)
94 .... 34. Routine fly in the "V"
96 .... 35. "Trouble" ball in the "V"
98 .... 36. Fly ball to left field
100 .... 37. Fly ball to right field
102 .... 38. Ground ball in the infield
104 .... 39. Base hit to the outfield
106 .... 40. Bunt
108 .... Review
109 .... **Runners at first and third**
   (See also cases 33-37 and 40)
110 .... 41. Pickoff throw to first
112 .... 42. Pickoff throw to third
114 .... 43. Second-base steal
116 .... 44. Fly ball & time play
118 .... 45. Ground ball to the base umpire's right
120 .... 46. Ground ball to the base umpire's left
122 .... 47. Base hit to the outfield
124 .... Review
125 .... **Runner at second base (See also case 23)**
126 .... 48. Third-base steal
128 .... 49. Fly ball in the "V"
130 .... 50. Fly ball to left field
132 .... 51. Fly ball to right field
134 .... 52. Ground ball in the infield
136 .... 53. Bunt
138 .... Review
139 ....**Runner at third base (See also cases 42, 44)**
140 .... 54. Stealing home!
142 .... 55. Fly ball in the "V"
144 .... 56. Fly ball to left field
146 .... 57. Fly ball to right field
148 .... 58. Ground ball in the infield
150 .... 59. Bunt
152 .... Review
153 .... **Runners at second and third**
   (See also cases 23, 42, 44)
154 .... 60. Stealing home!
156 .... 61. Fly ball in the "V"
158 .... 62. Fly ball to left field
160 .... 63. Fly ball to right field
162 .... 64. Ground ball in the infield
164 .... 65. Bunt
166 .... Review

ACKNOWLEDGMENTS

In its third printing, *Baseball Umpires Guidebook — Proper Positioning* is among the elite umpiring manuals in existence today. Many people have influenced the book to make it a success.

Mark Ambrosius is largely responsible for authoring the original work. His long hours and dedication to improving umpiring are reflected within these pages.

Jim Evans, a longtime AL umpire and operator of the Jim Evans' Academy of Professional Umpiring, served as the motivation for Ambrosius after he attended Evans' school. Ambrosius credits Evans for inspiring him to write the book.

Scott Ehret, former *Referee* editor, worked extensively on the first two editions of this book. His various experiences throughout his 30-plus years in umpiring improved the book immensely.

Dave Yeast, NCAA national coordinator of umpiring, helped me edit and update this third edition to incorporate mechanics and philosophies emphasized in amateur baseball.

Each of the men involved share a common goal — improved umpiring — and we thank them for their contributions.

— Bill Topp
Referee Editor

INTRODUCTION

"This manual has a simple purpose: To provide a framework for amateur baseball umpire training. The positions, mechanics and theories included on these pages are time-proven principles currently taught to and used by umpires in professional baseball's minor leagues, occasionally supplemented or altered to fit the situations unique to amateur games. These principles work because they consistently guide umpires to the proper position to see all of each play."

That paragraph was written by the original author of this book, Mark Ambrosius, in the first and second editions. In this third edition, those principles remain the same.

Time has proven we've reached two important audiences with this book: Veteran umpires who want a clean, solid reference work they can use as a refresher before and during each season; and, new umpires who are trying desperately to figure out where to stand and why.

Many associations have used this manual as the textbook for new-umpire training. We're confident that by using this manual, either as an individual or as a teacher, you and your fellow umpires will be better prepared for the wonderful (and sometimes wacky!) things that happen on the baseball field.

For the third edition, we've extended the scope of Ambrosius' work to include additional guidance for amateur umpires, specifically incorporating mechanics found mostly on college fields. Whether you're using professional, minor league mechanics, follow NCAA-prescribed procedures, or are influenced by NFHS mechanics, this book will offer you specific perspectives and guidelines to help you in your next games.

As with all of our *Referee* books, please let us know what you think. Your views help us shape future projects.

— Bill Topp
Referee Editor

Philosophy of Positioning

At any given moment during a game, each umpire assumes the position on the field that he believes will give him the best opportunity to rule correctly on the next play; as each play develops, each umpire adjusts his position to observe the ongoing action.

Two-man mechanics is a system of angles, distances, shared responsibilities and anticipation; the most important of these is anticipation. When you can reasonably predict what is *most likely* to happen next, you can establish your angle, cut the distance and meet your responsibilities; you can also move to the proper position before the play begins and adjust as the play develops.

Of course, you could wind up in the proper position merely by following the action, following the ball, or both. You could get to the right spot purely by accident, just because you have to be *someplace*. And in most situations you'd be lucky enough to see the play no matter where you are on the field — most plays don't really need an umpire. But when there is a decision to be made, your decision will be more accurate and will be accepted more readily if you are in a position to really see what happens.

If you've umpired for any amount of time, you've been told to "get in position" to make the call. That's good advice, even when it comes from angry players, coaches and fans who have no idea what that position is. It's the same advice this book offers, except here you'll get useful suggestions and the reasoning behind them. The suggestions will focus on helping you get into position in time to wait for the play to develop, because an umpire who can stand still and watch the action has a much better opportunity to rule accurately on that action.

While "get in position" is good advice, it is also incomplete. As you strive to be in the proper position to see a play, you must concentrate on seeing the entire play. Never look away from one play, hurrying to move to the next action, before you are *certain* the first play is over. Remember the sage advice offered by virtually every umpire training staff: "It ain't nothin' till I call it!"

Along with judgment, rules knowledge, concentration and courage, positioning is an important umpiring asset. When you are in a place on the field that offers an advantageous view of the action, your decision will be more confident, more often correct and more readily accepted by players, coaches and spectators.

So, learn the information on the pages that follow. Commit the pages to memory. But most importantly, understand the advantages of each position and its associated movement. When you understand why one position is better than another, you'll find yourself in great position throughout each game.

Theory of Proper Positioning

"Angle is primary; distance is secondary; closer is better, up to a point."

While no single sentence can really summarize everything you need to know about positioning, that one comes close. When you understand how angle, distance and proximity work together, you understand how your on-field position affects your opportunity to rule correctly on a given play. Let's consider each of the three elements.

Angle. Your line of sight must provide you with an opportunity to view an important, instantaneous activity (on a tag play) or combination of two activities (on a force play). To get the right line of sight, you have to establish the correct angle.

For decades, veteran umpires have preached to rookie umpires: Get the 90-degree angle. That's a wonderful starting point, if you understand what 90-degrees you are trying to get.

For example, on a tag play you would like to be looking at the space between the fielder's hand or glove (holding the ball) and the runner's body. Assume for a moment that the fielder has the ball and is waiting with his glove extended to tag the runner. As the runner slides, his movement establishes his line of action. Your standard "90-degree angle" would place your line of sight perpendicular to the runner's slide — a very good starting point. (You may have to adjust your angle to see over, under or around the fielder's body or the runner's body!)

Distance. In theory, once you establish the proper angle, you have a reasonable opportunity to accurately view the action, regardless of the distance between your position and the play. The theory holds as long as you do not have to adjust your angle.

In reality, the final moments of virtually every play require some amount of adjustment. The greater your distance from the play, the more difficult it will be to make that adjustment, but if you have not first established the proper angle your ability to adjust is inconsequential.

Proximity. How close you want to be to a developing play depends on several variables, including: the type of play, your mobility, your peripheral vision. Begin by moving to a position eight to 10 feet from a tag play; 12 to 15 feet from a force play. As you gain experience, adjust those distances to fit your own ability.

Mechanics of Positioning

The Plate Umpire

The plate umpire's initial position is the same on every play: behind the catcher. His first priority is always the same: rule each pitch a ball or strike. To be comfortable in the position and to accomplish the first priority, the plate umpire must develop a solid, functional stance. Assuming you will work with an chest protector inside your shirt, there are three stances to choose from: box, scissors and knee. If you work with an outside ("balloon," "raft") protector, you will work in the "square" stance.

Inside-protector work. Your fundamentals are the same, regardless of the stance you select: Assume a position behind the catcher looking between the catcher and the batter; you must be able to clearly see the pitcher, the entire plate and the batter's knees. To see all of those elements, it is important to move into "the slot" — that area between the catcher and the batter. The farther you are into the slot, the better you will see the strike zone.

Two additional factors have tremendous impact on your view of the strike zone: head height and stability. Your head should be positioned so the bottom of your chin is even with the top of the catcher's helmet. If you work with your head lower, your view of the knee-high pitch at or near the outside corner of the plate will be restricted.

To determine proper head height, use a dining room or folding chair to simulate a squatting catcher. Pretend the top of the chair back is the top of the catcher's head. Practice dropping into your stance until it is a crisp, one-motion movement. Working in front of a mirror is a great technique; so is the use of video tape, if you can find someone who will tape you setting into your slot position. If you have a partner, work on it together.

From the moment the pitcher releases a pitch until the ball arrives in the catcher's glove, your head should remain absolutely stable. If your head moves at all, your view of the strike zone will be blurred and your judgment will be inconsistent.

As you work to apply those fundamentals, consider the following stance information while you refer to the illustrations on pages 14 and 15:

Box — Your feet are spread slightly more than shoulder width apart; your feet are placed in a heel-toe configuration, with your slot foot (left foot for a right-handed batter) slightly ahead of your back foot and your weight evenly distributed on the balls of your feet. As the pitcher delivers, you will bend at the knees, keeping your shoulders square to the pitcher, and you will lean slightly forward, into the pitch, to establish your head height and stability. The box stance is the easiest for beginning umpires because it provides very good balance and it distributes stress evenly between the legs.

Scissors — Your legs will be fully open, similar to an open pair of scissors, with your feet directly behind each other one full stride apart. Your slot foot (left foot for a right-handed batter) is positioned approximately six inches behind the catcher's inside foot; your back leg is fully extended, knee straight, with the ball of the foot on the ground and the heel elevated. When the pitcher delivers, your slot-leg knee is bent at a 90-degree angle; the vast majority of your weight is on your bent leg; keeping your shoulders square to the pitcher, you will lean forward dramatically into the pitch and establish your head height and stability. The scissors stance is very difficult for beginning umpires because it provides poor balance and (due to the high number of right-handed batters) it places extreme stress on the left leg. By forcing you to lean forward dramatically, it also exposes your shoulder and collar-bone areas to potential injury.

Knee — The knee stance is similar to the scissors, but with several advantages. Your feet will be directly behind each other, about one-half stride apart. Your slot foot (left foot for right-handed batters) is positioned approximately six inches behind the catcher's inside foot; your back knee will be on the ground. As the pitcher delivers, keep your shoulder square to the pitcher and your back essentially straight, but lean forward slightly to establish your head height and stability. The knee stance is fairly easy to learn, provides good balance and excellent stability, but places heavy stress on the left leg (standing up after each pitch) and can hinder the plate umpire's movement reacting to batted balls.

Outside-protector work. Although generally discarded by umpires with two or three years of experience (in favor of an inside protector), the outside protector is favored by beginning umpires for its superior level of protection. It is also the protector generally provided for umpires by recreation departments and youth leagues.

With an outside protector, you will *not* work in the slot. The protector is simply too bulky to allow that position. Instead, you will work directly above the catcher's head. Your chin must be well above the catcher's helmet to provide a clear view of the bottom of the strike zone.

To determine proper head height, use a dining room or folding chair to simulate a squatting catcher. Pretend the top of the chair back is the top of the catcher's head. Practice dropping into your stance until it is a crisp, one-motion movement. Working in front of a mirror is a great technique; so is the use of video tape, if you can find some one who will tape you setting into your slot position. If you have a partner, work on it together.

Square stance — Your feet will be spread slightly more than shoulder width apart and will be placed on a direct line, perpendicular to a line from home plate to the pitcher's rubber. You should be about one-half step behind the catcher. As the pitcher delivers, keep your shoulders square to the pitcher, flex your knees slightly, and bend slightly forward to establish your head height and stability. Be certain you press the top of the protector firmly against the underside of your chin in order to provide protection for your throat area. The square stance is very easy for beginning umpires because it provides good balance and stability. In addition, the outside protector, properly placed against the underside of the chin, provides unparalleled protection. The drawbacks: Many umpires find the outside protector both clumsy and cumbersome as they move to cover the infield, and a number of umpires attempt to work the slot area while using the outside protector. Avoid the temptation because the bulk of the protector will prevent any hope of a good view of the outside portion of the strike zone.

Practicing your stance. You can practice your stance without being on a baseball diamond. In fact, it is a good idea to try these practice techniques and to become comfortable with the movement before you take the field.

For example, here is a simple practice method for the box stance (you can adapt the equipment to the scissors or knee stance on your own):

Get two pairs of shoes and two yard sticks (or any straight sticks, or even rope, about three to four feet long). Place one pair of shoes where a batter would stand in the batter's box. Place the second pair where a catcher's feet would normally be when set to receive a pitch. Place one of the sticks in a straight line, parallel to the pitcher's rubber, behind the heels of the "catcher," toward the batter. Place the toes of your slot foot on this stick. Place the second stick parallel to the first stick behind the heel of your slot foot. Place the toes of your back foot on the second stick, slightly more than shoulder width from your slot foot. Now turn the back foot out, about 30- to 45-degrees away from your slot foot. This will keep you from "kneeing" the catcher when you squat. Make sure the toes of your slot foot are pointed directly at the pitcher, so foul balls and wild pitches will carom off the steel toe of your shoe instead of the side of your foot.

Place your slot arm across your waist with your elbow tucked close to your side. Your other hand should grasp the top of your thigh, elbow tucked tightly against your side. These arm positions will help protect the bones in your arms from pitched and foul balls, which can cause serious injury.

Focusing on the pitched ball. Practice getting into your set position until you can drop into your stance smoothly and crisply. Have someone "soft toss" a rolled-up pair of white socks, underhand into the strike zone. Follow the ball with just your eyes all the way in and through the zone. Have your partner, who is tossing the ball, watch closely to see if your head moves or if you are drifting into or away from the pitch. Make sure the soft toss drill includes pitches that are up, down and near each of the corners. Have your partner note which pitches cause you to move and when you stay stable. Work on the pitches where movement is a problem.

Do not be concerned with calling balls and strikes until you can remain absolutely stable and follow the ball with only your eyes. Again, this practice exercise is

well suited for a video camera. You will see yourself drift or move, even though you probably will not feel the movement.

With the marking sticks still in place, step back from the slot position, as you would when the ball is being returned to the pitcher. Get back into your slot position and proper foot position for several pitches. Practice getting into and out of the slot until you can place your feet into position without having to look down at them. Practice the "soft toss" with the chair, until you can sit down in your set position crisply, without having to check if your head is positioned at the proper height.

Practicing these techniques, either in front of a mirror or with the aid of a video camera, will enhance your ability to get into the slot and will help your confidence — in your calls and in yourself.

Here comes the pitch. As the ball approaches the plate, focus your eyes on the ball and follow it all the way to the catcher's glove *moving only your eyes*. Head movement is not permissible! Moving your head will "push" the ball away from you and you will not see the location of the pitch accurately. By following the flight of the ball with only your eyes, you will accurately record the pitch location.

Here is an easy-to-understand parallel: If you suddenly jerk a camera the instant you press the shutter, the picture will be blurred and out of focus. This principle is the same when you view a pitch approaching the plate. If you keep your head still and follow the ball with only your eyes, you will see the pitch and it's location much better.

You must follow the ball, in flight, all the way to the catcher's glove. Read the location of the pitch and read the catcher's glove location when he catches the ball. Stay in your stance until you have seen the pitch and determined whether it is a strike or a ball.

Timing is critical on the pitched ball. Watch the ball with your eyes all the way to the glove, and watch the catcher catch the ball. Then make up your mind on the ball's location and call the pitch: ball or strike.

If you decide the pitch is a ball, stay in your stance and say, "Ball," while keeping your eyes still focused on the ball. If you decide the pitch is a strike, stand straight up and call, "Strike," while still keeping your head and eyes on the ball. Dropped third strikes and trapped foul tips are easily missed when plate umpires fly out of the plate area to emphasize a called strike. Work on proper mechanics first. After three or four seasons, develop an individual style that incorporates these sound mechanics. Staying down on balls and rising upright on strikes will help convince players, coaches and fans that you are confident of your decisions.

Making Adjustments. If every catcher and every batter positioned themselves exactly the same on every pitch, your job as plate umpire would be easy. You could establish a "groove" in the slot, sit down in the same spot every time, and call all the pitches. In reality, it doesn't happen. Catchers will "squeeze" the inside corner for their pitchers and take away your slot space. Batters will crowd the plate and take more of that space

Box profile view

Box front view

Scissors profile view

Scissors front view

Knee profile view

Knee front view

Square profile view

Square front view

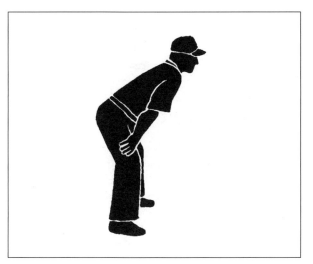

Hands-on-knees set profile view

Hands-on-knees set front view

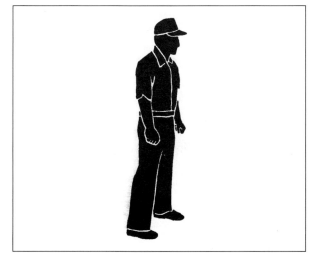

Standing set profile view

Standing set front view

from you. Some catchers, especially those with little experience, work high and block your view of the plate.

As you gain experience, you'll read these situations and make adjustments to your slot position to accommodate calling balls and strikes in these situations (no adjustment needed for umpires working with the outside protector because they do not work in the slot). Remember, the most important thing is to keep your head stable so you can see the plate area. If a catcher's position takes this view away, adjust. Your first adjustment is up. You work higher above the catcher's head when he crowds the inside corner. This will allow you to look down onto the plate area. This may take away the low strike from the pitcher, but your aim is to see as much of the plate as possible. This adjustment will improve your view of the plate, compared to the view you would have if you made no adjustment.

The second adjustment you can make on a catcher who sets up inside is to move farther into the slot, toward the batter. This will increase your viewing angle to the plate and reopen the plate area (and strike zone). This move pushes the outside-corner pitch farther outside, but again, your goal is to see as much of the strike zone as possible.

Never move to the catcher's outside shoulder.

The Base Umpire

Depending on the game situation, the base umpire may be stationed behind the first baseman just outside the first-base line, or on the infield grass on the first-base or the third-base side behind the mound. When and where you begin each play is illustrated in the case studies that follow, but a summary of the information is below:

No runners on base (Position A). Stand with your right foot just outside the first-base line, 10 to 12 feet behind the first baseman. Adjust your depth to the first baseman's position, forward if he plays near the grass and back if he is deep toward the outfield. Your position should allow you to get into the infield without interfering with the first baseman. Your shoulders should be square to home plate with your feet comfortably apart in a standing set. When the pitcher makes contact with the rubber, come to a hands-on-knees set. Watch the pitcher deliver the ball and change your focus to the batter as the ball approaches the plate; be ready to help your partner on the half swing.

*Working from Position A is the **only** time the base umpire may go to the outfield to rule on a "trouble" ball. **Never** go to the outfield from Position B or C!*

Runner at first base (Position B). Stand half way between the mound and second base, straddling a line from the corner of home plate through the edge of the dirt on the first-base side of the mound. Your shoulders should be square to home plate. Before the pitcher contacts the rubber you should be in a standing set. When the pitcher contacts the rubber, come to a hands-on-knees set. Keep your eyes on the pitcher for balk

violations, then focus on the plate area as the ball crosses the plate; be ready to help your partner on the half swing. If the pitch is not hit, return to a standing set. Glance at the runner between pitches and be alert for a pickoff or delayed steal. If the ball is hit, remember: Step up, turn and face the ball.

Runners at first and second; runner at second; or, runner at third (Position C): Stand half way between the mound and second base, straddling a line from the corner of home plate through the edge of the dirt on the third-base side of the mound. Your shoulders should be square to home plate. Before the pitcher contacts the rubber you should be in a standing set. When the pitcher contacts the rubber, come to a hands-on-knees set. Keep your eyes focused on the pitcher for balk violations; if third base is empty, as the pitcher releases the ball glance briefly over your right shoulder at R2 to see if he is stealing; focus on the plate area as the ball reaches the plate; be ready to help your partner on the half swing. If the pitch is not hit and no runner is stealing, return to a standing set. Glance at the runner between pitches and be alert for a pickoff or delayed steal. If the ball is hit, remember: Step up, turn and face the ball.

Runners at first and third; runners at second and third; bases loaded (Position C): Position C provides better coverage for double plays and double steals.

Stand half way between the mound and second base, straddling a line from the corner of home plate through the edge of the dirt on the third-base side of the mound. Your shoulders should be square to home plate. Before the pitcher contacts the rubber you should be in a standing set. When the pitcher contacts the rubber, come to a hands-on-knees set. Keep your eyes on the pitcher for balk violations, then focus on the plate area as the ball crosses the plate; be ready to help your partner on the half swing. If the pitch is not hit and no runner is stealing, return to a standing set. Glance at the runner between pitches and be alert for a pickoff or delayed steal. If the ball is hit, remember: Step up, turn and face the ball.

Work on these starting positions. From them you will be able to get to the positions listed in the case studies. If you do not start in the right place, it is very difficult to finish in the right place. Remember: Read the play as it happens and hustle to your next position. Infield plays often happen very quickly. Proper positioning helps you be where you can see the entire play develop and make the proper call.

Step up, turn and face the ball. One fundamental movement for base umpires is: Step up, turn and face the ball. It is the initial move that follows almost every hit, and is followed in turn by "pause, read and react." But you will not step up, turn and face the ball properly on the field unless you practice the movement off the field.

Stand in a room, in your back yard or anywhere, and assume your hands-on-knees set. Your feet should be comfortably apart, slightly wider than shoulder width. Flex at the knees and "sit down" into your stance, leaning forward *slightly,* bending at the waist. In a good hands-on-knees set, you should be able to look forward comfortably; if you bend too far, you will have to strain your neck muscles to avoid looking down at the ground.

Have someone throw a ball to your left or to your right. When they begin the throw, pretend it is a batter beginning his stride to the ball. You should anticipate a batted ball and shift your weight to the balls of your feet. As the ball is thrown to your left or to your right, step up with the foot nearest the ball. For example, on a ball "hit to right field," your first step up would be with your left foot. Turn and pivot on that foot to face the ball. Reading the fielders from this position will allow you to make your next move smoothly.

Practice moving to your left and to your right, coming to a complete stop, and dropping to a hands-on-knees set. This "move, stop and set" pattern will be important on the field; if it is "automatic" before your first game you'll be off to a good start.

Definition of terms

The following terms are used throughout the positioning case studies that follow. Although many of the terms will seem self-explanatory, a brief review will insure complete understanding.

B1 — The batter, also referred to as BR (batter-runner).

Below the knee — The phrase is used frequently as a catch-all to describe a difficult catch, usually made in the outfield. A catch that is made "below the knee" is one which requires the covering umpire to signal the successful catch and (at times) verbally confirm, "That's a catch!"; or, to signal "safe" and verbally confirm, "No catch! No catch!" Consider that a catch is "below the knee" whenever the fielder: actually reaches down below his knee; dives to make the play; falls before or after the ball arrives; makes a catch with his back turned to the infield; collides with another fielder as or immediately after reaching the ball.

The Box — That area in fair territory bordered by home plate, the 45-foot line, the pitcher's mound and the mid-point of the third-base line. The Box is approximately 45 feet by 45 feet square. When a batted ball is fielded within The Box and a play develops at first base, BU should strive for a position near the first-base cutout to observe the play.

BU — The base umpire. UIC is the Umpire in Chief, the plate umpire. When more than two umpires work together, U1 is the first base umpire, U2 is the second base umpire and U3 is the third base umpire.

Chest to the ball — Each umpire wants to maintain a position with the ball within his field of view. By keeping your chest pointed toward the ball, you'll keep the play in front of you. Although exceptions exist, when in doubt turn your chest to the ball.

Clear the catcher — The plate umpire (UIC) will clear the catcher whenever a play follows a pitch. To clear the catcher, step back with your back foot (right foot with a right-handed batter, left foot with a left-handed batter) first. That will increase the distance between your body and the catcher. Next, step with your opposite foot and move to your left, back from or around the catcher.

Clear the runner — At the conclusion of any play which requires the UIC to cover a runner's safe advance to a base, the base umpire (BU) must assume responsibility for that runner, thus releasing the UIC who must return to his normal position. Before he can "clear the runner," the UIC will wait for the BU to take responsibility for all runners by saying, "Okay, I've got the runners." At that time, the UIC can move out of the infield, into foul territory and assume his position at home plate.

Cutout in the infield — On diamonds with grass infields, the area adjacent to each base includes a semi-circular area of dirt extending approximately 13 feet from the base. The area where that dirt infringes on the grass infield is called the "cutout." An umpire who is at the cutout is approximately 12-15 feet from the play.

Fielders — The defensive players, routinely designated by their numerical scorekeeping identifying numbers: F1 is the pitcher, F2 is the catcher, F3 is the first baseman, etc.

First-base line extended — An imaginary line that extends the first-base fair/foul line into foul territory behind home plate an unlimited distance. The UIC will assume a position on the first-base line extended in several instances including: to render fair/foul decisions on batted balls to the right of home plate; to observe action at first base as another runner scores; on selected tag plays at home plate.

45-foot line — The 45-foot line, which is three feet long and is drawn at a 90-degree angle to the first-base line 45 feet from home plate, marks the beginning of the runner's lane. That's important for players; but the same line is *tremendously* important for base umpires. It is a visible benchmark for several position adjustments, as is illustrated in the case studies that follow.

Glance at the runner — Although umpires are advised to "keep your eye everlastingly on the ball," you will find it necessary to glance at the runner on several occasions, including: as each runner tags up or touches each base, whenever a runner and fielder pass within close proximity (to observe obstruction or interference), and to monitor a runner's progress as a play develops.

"Go" or "goes" — Under a variety of circumstances, BU may be required to "go," physically entering the outfield-grass area. If there are no runners on base, BU

"goes" to rule catch/no catch on a "trouble" ball and to determine fair/foul on a batted ball in flight down the right-field line.

Opening the gate — A basic umpire's movement which allows continued observation of a batted or thrown ball as the ball passes the umpire. To "open the gate," begin in an upright stance with your feet comfortably apart; keeping your chest to the ball, take an initial step backward while pointing your foot toward the ball's destination; as or before the ball passes your location, turn by stepping with your opposite foot and focus on the developing play. "Opening the gate" is similar to "clearing the catcher."

Pause, read and react — A three-step method which, when properly employed, will help you determine where you should go and what your responsibilities will be during a developing play. "Pause" — take a moment to observe the initial action; "Read" — determine what play is going to develop and what position adjustment you should make; "React" — move into position for the anticipated play and, as appropriate, communicate your intentions to your partner. "Pause, read and react" is particularly important in coordinating two-man umpiring coverage. It insures that the umpires identically evaluate each developing play.

Play — The action that develops as a runner, the ball and a fielder arrive at the same place at approximately the same time. A play usually occurs at or near a base and normally requires an umpire's decision. As the umpire, you *must* move to a play only when all three elements are coming together.

Pivot — The three-step movement used by BU as he moves into the infield from position A. When a batted ball is hit to the outfield, BU will pivot to observe the batter-runner's touch of first base, anticipating the batter-runner's advance toward second. A proper pivot occurs on the infield grass, one or two steps from the edge of the first-base cutout; it includes planting the left foot, turning the body counter-clockwise on the right foot as the batter-runner reaches first base, and stepping briskly with the left foot toward second base as the batter-runner continues around first.

Position A — BU's position at the start of each inning and whenever a play begins with no runners on base. Position A is near the first-base line, standing with both feet in foul territory, at least 15-18 feet beyond first base and at least two steps behind the first baseman.

Position B — BU's position on the first-base side of the middle of the infield. Position B is approximately midway between the pitcher's mound and second base, just to the first-base side of the mound. His feet should straddle an imaginary line drawn from home plate through the edge of the dirt circle of the mound. When

the pitcher takes his stance on the mound the base umpire should be in a hands-on-knees set, shoulders square and chest facing directly to home plate. BU will be in position B when there is a runner on first base only, when there are runners on first and third, when there are runners at second and third, and when the bases are loaded.

Position C — BU's position on the third-base side of the middle of the infield. Position C is approximately midway between the pitcher's mound and second base, just to the third-base side of the mound. His feet should straddle an imaginary line drawn from home plate through the edge of the dirt circle of the mound. When the pitcher takes his stance on the mound the base umpire should be in a hands-on-knees set, shoulders square and chest facing directly to home plate. BU will begin in position C whenever a runner is on second base and third base is not occupied, and when there is a runner at third base only.

Read the throw — As a play develops, you must judge the quality of the throw. In general, if a throw is "good" you will maintain your initial position to observe the developing play; if the throw is "bad" you will have to adjust your position according to the throw.

Release runner to third — When the UIC verbally informs BU, "I've got third if he comes" or "I've got third if he tags," BU will observe the touch or tag-up at second base, then release responsibility for that runner to UIC and assume responsibility for plays made on other (trailing) runners.

Runners — Players from the team at bat are identified by their locations on base at the beginning of a play or sequence of plays: R1 is the runner who starts a scenario at first base, R2 at second, R3 at third.

Runner's lane — The three-foot-wide lane, beginning at the 45-foot line and extending to first base. A batter-runner is innocent of *unintentional* interference with a fielder covering first base if he advances to first with both feet stepping on or inside the lines of the lane.

Set for the play — You must come to a complete stop before the critical moment of any play and remain stationary until you make your decision. Just like a camera taking a picture, your eyes must be stationary to produce a clear image. To keep your eyes stationary, your body must come to a complete stop as the tag or force play occurs.

Set positions — There are two used by base umpires.
   Hands-on-knees set: With your feet slightly more than shoulder width apart, squat and lean forward slightly, and place your hands on your knees. Keep your back straight and your head up, looking at the play. Your arms should lock firmly to keep your head still and allow you to see the play. Use the hands-on-

knees set prior to each pitch when you are in position B or C, and at your discretion as plays develop (alternative as plays develop: standing set).

Standing set: With your feet comfortably apart, keep your shoulders square to the play. Your knees should be slightly bent but your body remains upright with your hands at your sides. Do not use the standing set position prior to a pitch when you are in position B or C; use it at your discretion in position A and as plays develop.

Square to the bag — When set for a play at any base, your head, shoulders and feet should be in line and perpendicular to a line from your location to the base. By taking a position square to the bag, you will avoid a tendency to turn away from the play before it is complete.

Step up, turn and face the ball — A three-step movement used by BU in position B or C when the ball is hit. Using your foot nearest where the ball is hit, take one step forward; turn or pivot and move, chest to the ball; determine your next move or responsibility and execute.

Third-base line extended — An imaginary line that extends the third-base fair/foul line into foul territory behind home plate an unlimited distance. The UIC will assume a position on the third-base line extended in several instances including: to render fair/foul decisions on batted balls to the left of home plate; to observe a runner touching third base as another runner scores; on selected tag plays at home plate.

Trouble ball — A batted ball hit to the outfield that will present a problem for the fielder. Examples: A fly ball that forces the left or right fielder to charge toward the foul line; a fly ball that forces an outfielder to charge straight in; a fly ball at which two or more fielders converge; any batted ball that will require a fair/foul decision in the outfield. When a trouble ball is identified in your area of responsibility, you must communicate with your partner, indicating which umpire will take the fair/foul and catch/no catch decisions. Use the "pause, read and react" method to identify and respond to a trouble ball.

UIC — The Umpire in Chief; the plate umpire. BU is the base umpire. When more than two umpires work together, U1 is the first base umpire, U2 is the second base umpire and U3 is the third base umpire.

Case Studies

On the following pages you will find discussions of the most typical baseball plays, divided into sections according to the eight basic runner configurations that occur in most games:

Bases empty
Runner at first base
Runners at first and second
Bases loaded
Runners at first and third
Runner at second base
Runner at third base
Runners at second and third

In all, there are more than 60 combinations, but there's no reason to feel overwhelmed. As you study the various cases, you'll begin to see a pattern of positions, responsibilities and movement for each umpire. As the patterns become familiar, you may even find yourself predicting what's coming next.

However, resist any temptation you might feel to skim through these pages. They are the "meat" of two-man positioning. Many of the case studies will reveal subtle aspects of positioning and movement — two of the essential ingredients of exceptional umpiring. When you know what to expect, you'll be prepared to cope with the plays that are about to occur.

Each section of case plays details responsibilities in a specific runner configuration. The sections begin with a discussion of factors each umpire should consider before a play begins. For the base umpire that includes: basic position, factors which might lead to adjustments in the basic position, and events which may occur in order of priority. For the plate umpire that includes: response to playing action that can easily be anticipated, and events which may occur in order of priority.

Each case study is broken down into several elements.

• The first page includes: game situation; an actual play under discussion; and, the base and plate umpires' responsibilities and movements, presented in sequence. (To keep the list of explanations and duties parallel, an umpire's list often "skips" one or more numbers. That indicates his partner has multiple tasks to accomplish before the umpire under discussion is expected to do anything.) There is also space allocated for your own notes and any questions you might want to discuss with a partner, your class instructor or — if you are an NASO member — with baseball experts on the NASO Hotline.

• Page two of the case study presents a diagram outlining the recommended starting positions for the umpires and the movements they would logically employ during the playing action.

At the end of each of the eight basic configurations, there is a one-page review of positioning factors and a true-false quiz covering each umpire's responsibilities.

Runner configuration: Bases empty

Base umpire position: Position A

Adjustment factors:

First baseman's defensive position: If F3 is playing near the foul line, move deeper to give him plenty of room to field a batted ball; if F3 is playing unusually deep, be certain you are at least two steps farther from home plate than he is; if F3 is playing off the line or forward toward home plate, you can adjust your position by moving closer to first base, but be sure you are at least 15 feet from the bag so you maintain the perspective you may need to rule fair/foul on a bouncing ball near the base.

Batter-runner tendencies: If B1 is "built for speed" (short, slim, sprinter's body), consider adjusting several feet toward home plate, anticipating a bunt; if B1 is a left-handed pull hitter, consider adjusting several feet away from home plate and/or one-half to one-full step farther into foul territory, for your safety.

In order of importance, be prepared for the following situations:

1. An illegal pitch.
2. Help for the plate umpire on the check-swing.
3. Batted ball that travels beyond first base — rule fair or foul at or near the right-field line.
4. A "trouble ball" in your area of the outfield — beginning with any ball hit directly to F8 and extending through right field to dead-ball territory outside the right-field line.
5. A ground ball in the infield: You have the play on B1 at first base and any play that develops at first, second and third.
6. A batted or bunted ball with F3, F1 and B1 all converging at the base.
7. "Pressure" from the second baseman.
8. A clean hit, or any batted ball to UIC's area of the outfield.

Plate umpire anticipation:

Your initial position is always behind the plate. As the pitcher begins his delivery, come set in your stance. Your initial responsibility is always calling the pitch a strike or a ball. Respond to the batted ball and the action as it develops.

Batted ball in the infield: Determine fair/foul on any batted ball to the third-base side, and on a batted ball to the first-base side if the ball does not physically pass the base; trail B1 toward first base, attempting to reach the 45-foot line (set before the play occurs) to observe the action at first base and to assist (if necessary) with a swipe tag or pulled foot; cover dead-ball areas in case of errant throw.

Batted ball to the outfield: You have responsibility for any ball that takes F8 toward left field, all balls hit to left field and the dead-ball area outside the left-field line. To left field: move into infield and rule fair/foul, catch/no catch as necessary. To right field: trail B1 toward first base; if BU "goes" on the hit, cover B1 at first, second and third as the play develops; if BU pivots, rule fair/foul and catch/no catch as necessary.

In order of importance, be prepared for the following situations:

1. An illegal pitch.
2. The pitch: ball or strike.
3. Check-swings and defensive appeals.
4. Slow-rolling ball down either base line: fair/foul from home plate to either bag.
5. A fair/foul call down the third-base or left-field line, or between home plate and first base.
6. A "trouble" ball in your area of the outfield — beginning with any ball hit to the center fielder's right and extending to the dead-ball area outside the left-field line.
7. A bunted ball when opponents converge — interference/obstruction.

Case Study 1 — Routine fly ball to right field

Game situation: Nobody on base

Action on the field: Fly ball to the right-field side of the center fielder

RESPONSIBILITIES

Base umpire	Plate umpire
1. Pause, read and react. Read the position of the fielder making the play and determine whether this is a ball in your coverage area (it is) and whether this is a "trouble" ball (it is not).	1. Pause, read and react. Read the developing play *and your partner*. If U1 "goes," observe B1's progress around the bases; if U1 pivots, observe the play on the batted ball.
2. Since it is not a "trouble" ball: Pivot, observing B1's touch of first base, and be ready for B1 to advance toward second.	
3. Continue to observe B1's progress until your partner determines a catch.	
	4. If there is a catch, inform your partner ("Bill, that's a catch."). If the ball is a hit, prepare to support your partner in a rundown between first and second. If R1 commits to third base, UIC returns to home.
5. If the ball is a hit, you have primary responsibility for B1 whether he advances to second, third or retreats to first.	

Notes

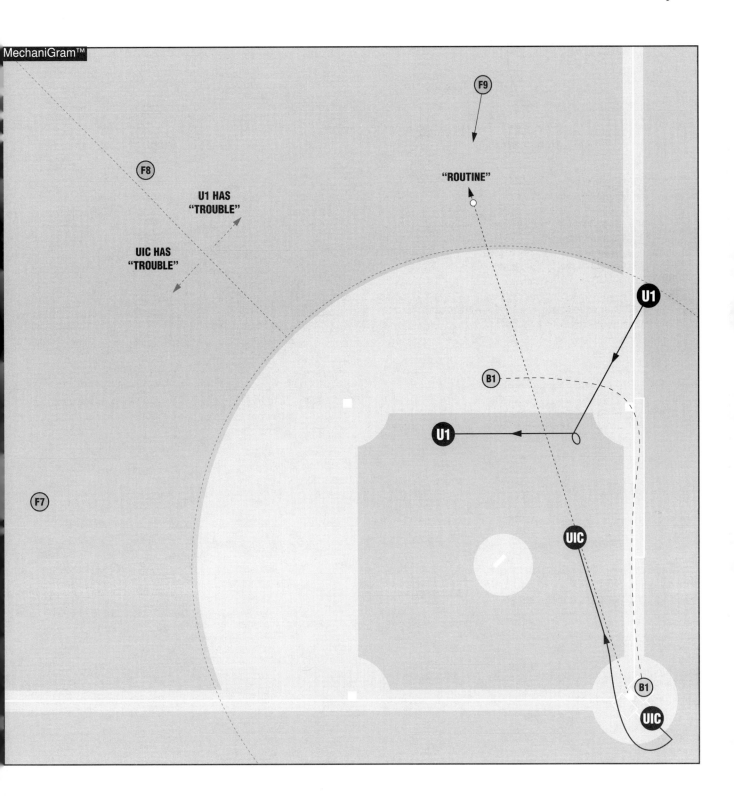

MechaniGram™

F9

F8

"ROUTINE"

U1 HAS
"TROUBLE"

UIC HAS
"TROUBLE"

U1

B1

U1

F7

UIC

B1

UIC

Case Study 2 — Routine fly ball to left field

Game situation: Nobody on base

Action on the field: Fly ball to the left-field side of the center fielder

RESPONSIBILITIES

Base umpire	Plate umpire
1. Pause, read and react. Read the position of the fielder making the play and determine whether this is a ball in your coverage area (it is not).	1. Pause, read and react. Read the position of the fielder making the play and determine whether this is a ball in your coverage area (it is) and whether this is a "trouble" ball (it is not).
2. Since it is not a ball in your coverage area: Pivot, observing B1's touch of first base, and be ready for B1 to advance toward second.	2. Since the ball is in your coverage area, move in the general direction of the developing play. If fair/foul is a consideration, move aggressively along the third-base line, set before the play occurs and rule fair or foul.
3. Continue to observe B1's progress until your partner determines a catch.	3. Develop the best angle possible to observe the catch/no catch.
5. If the ball is a hit, you have complete responsibility for B1 whether he advances to second, to third or retreats to first.	4. If there is a catch, inform your partner ("Bill, that's a catch."). If the ball is a hit, prepare to support your partner as necessary. If R1 commits to third base, UIC returns to home.

Notes

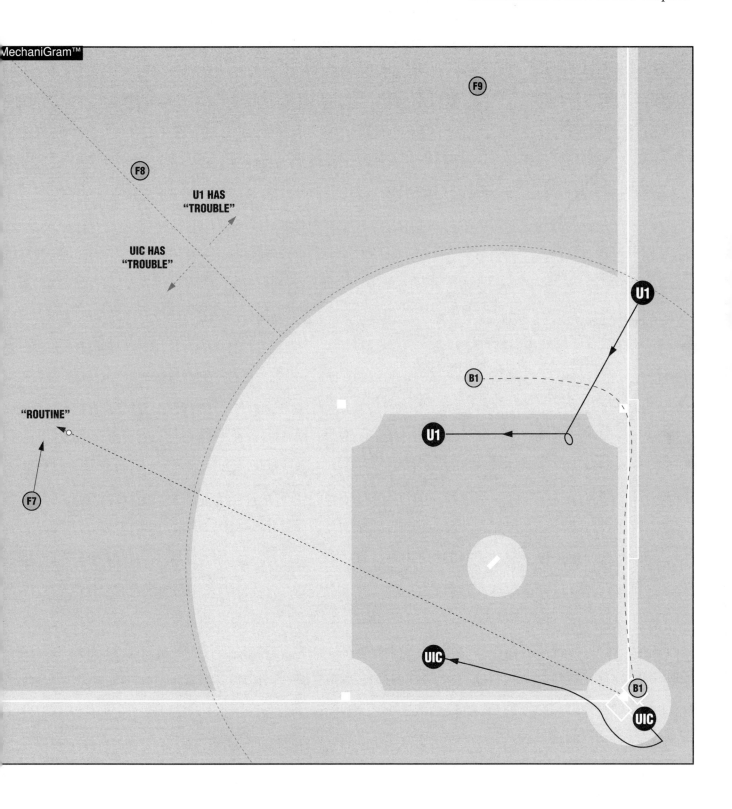

Case Study 3 — "Trouble" ball to right field

Game situation: Nobody on base

Action on the field: Fly ball to the right-field side of the center fielder

RESPONSIBILITIES

Base umpire	Plate umpire
1. Pause, read and react. Read the position of the fielder making the play and determine whether this is a ball in your coverage area (it is) and whether this is a "trouble" ball (it is).	1. Pause, read and react. Read the developing play *and your partner*. If U1 "goes," observe B1's progress around the bases; if U1 pivots, observe the play on the batted ball.
2. Since it is a "trouble" ball in your area, communicate to your partner ("Jeff, I'm going out!") and "go."	
3. If fair/foul is a consideration, move aggressively along the first-base line, set before the play occurs and rule fair or foul.	3. When U1 "goes," take a path on the right side of the infield and move midway between the pitcher's mound and first base to observe B1's touch of the base. After B1 passes first base, look to your partner and determine whether he has ruled a catch.
4. Develop the best angle possible to observe the catch/no catch. That will be as close as possible to a 90-degree angle between your line of sight and the path of the ball toward the fielder's glove.	
5. If there is a catch, signal only if the catch is made "below the knee"; verbally inform your partner of a routine catch. If a difficult play results in no catch, signal "safe" and verbally call, "No catch! No catch!"	
6. If the ball is a hit, continue to observe the outfield play until the ball is thrown to the infield. If it is an extra-base hit, move aggressively through foul territory toward home plate and attempt to support your partner by taking any play that develops at the plate.	6. If the ball is a hit, you have responsibility for B1 whether he returns to first base or advances to second, third and home. Your path will take you behind the mound, then toward third base as you remain ahead of B1.
	7. If B1 attempts to score, be alert for U1 to assume responsibility for the play at the plate. If U1 does not inform you he is taking the play, you have the play at the plate.
8. When playing action concludes, move into the infield to a position to observe B1 and communicate with UIC ("I've got the runner.").	8. When playing action concludes, continue to observe B1 until you can clear the runner by communicating with U1.

Notes

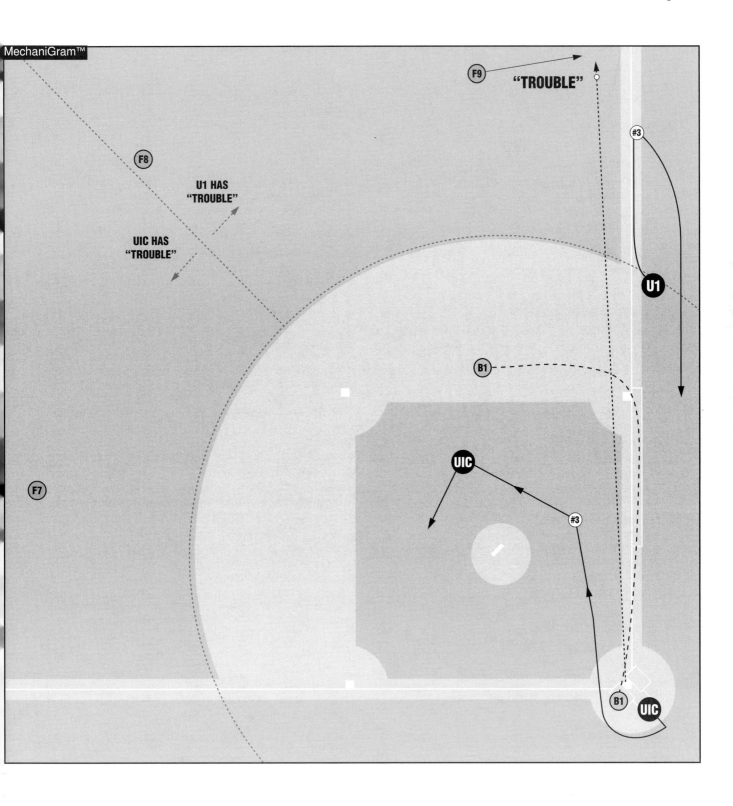

Case Study 4 — "Trouble" ball to left field

Game situation: Nobody on base

Action on the field: Fly ball to the left-field side of the center fielder

RESPONSIBILITIES

Base umpire	Plate umpire
1. Pause, read and react. Read the position of the fielder making the play and determine whether this is a ball in your coverage area (it is not).	1. Pause, read and react. Read the position of the fielder making the play and determine whether this is a ball in your coverage area (it is) and whether this is a "trouble" ball (it is).
2. Since it is not a ball in your coverage area: Pivot, observing B1's touch of first base, and be ready for B1 to advance toward second.	2. Because it is a "trouble" ball in your coverage area, move aggressively toward the developing play. If fair/foul is a consideration, remain along the third-base line, set before the play occurs and rule fair or foul.
3. Continue to observe B1's progress until your partner determines a catch.	3. Proceed as far as possible toward the play as you move to the best angle possible to observe the catch/no catch. That will be as close as possible to a 90-degree angle between your line of sight and the path of the ball toward the fielder's glove (since you are starting from behind home plate, you will not get very close to 90 degrees).
5. If the ball is a hit, you have complete responsibility for B1 whether he advances to second or retreats to first.	4. If there is a catch, signal only if the catch is made "below the knee"; verbally inform your partner of any catch ("Bill, that's a catch."). If the ball is a hit, prepare to support your partner as necessary.

Notes

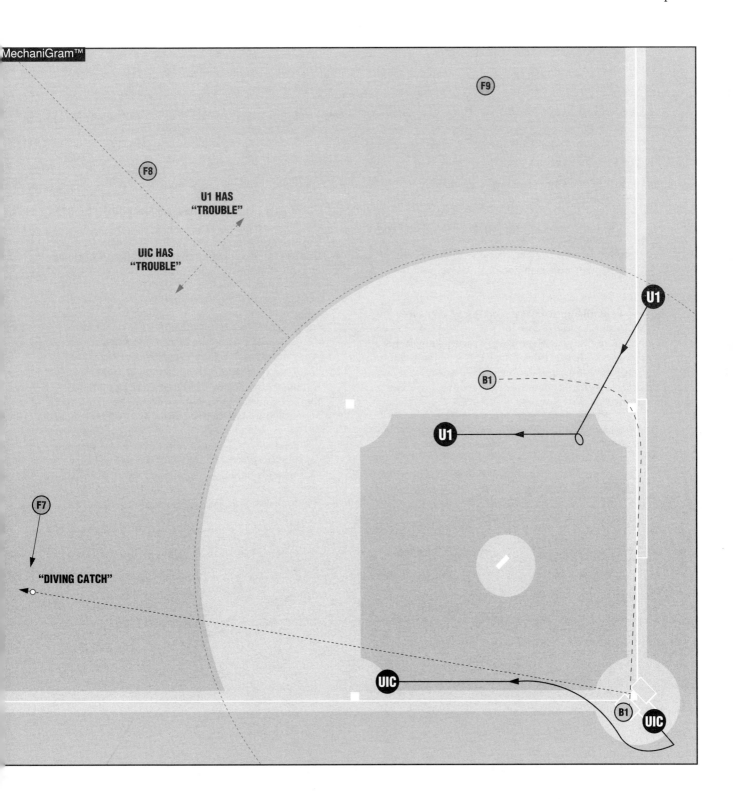

MechaniGram™

F9

F8

U1 HAS
"TROUBLE"

UIC HAS
"TROUBLE"

B1

U1

F7

"DIVING CATCH"

UIC

B1

UIC

Case Study 5 — Ground ball to the left side

Game situation: Nobody on base

Action on the field: Ground ball fielded by F4, F5 or F6

RESPONSIBILITIES

Base umpire	Plate umpire
1. Pause, read and react. Read the position of the fielder making the play.	1. Pause, read and react. Read the developing play. If fair/foul is not a factor, clear the catcher and move out to the catcher's left, then trail B1 toward first. If fair/foul is a factor, clear the catcher and establish a position straddling the first-base line or the first-base line extended, set before the play occurs and rule fair or foul.
2. Move to a fair-territory location 12 to 15 feet from first base.	
3. Establish a position two or three steps off the foul line.	
4. Read the throw. On a good throw, come to your set position and focus on the play at first base. On a bad throw, adjust: Move toward the foul line if the throw is wide toward home plate; move toward the first-base cutout if the throw is wide toward right field; lock in and concentrate on your timing if the throw is high or low.	4. Read the throw. On a good throw, continue trailing B1 toward first base, strive to reach the 45-foot line and set. On a bad throw, prepare for a swipe tag, pulled foot or an overthrow.
5. Observe B1's touch of first and listen for the ball to hit F3's glove.	5. As the play at first develops, come to a standing set and observe the play. Offer your opinion of a swipe tag or pulled foot only if U1 requests help.
6. *Timing!* Do not rule B1 out unless you are certain F3 has complete control of the ball. If the play breaks down and you are uncertain of a swipe tag or pulled foot, communicate with UIC *before* you rule B1 safe or out.	

Notes

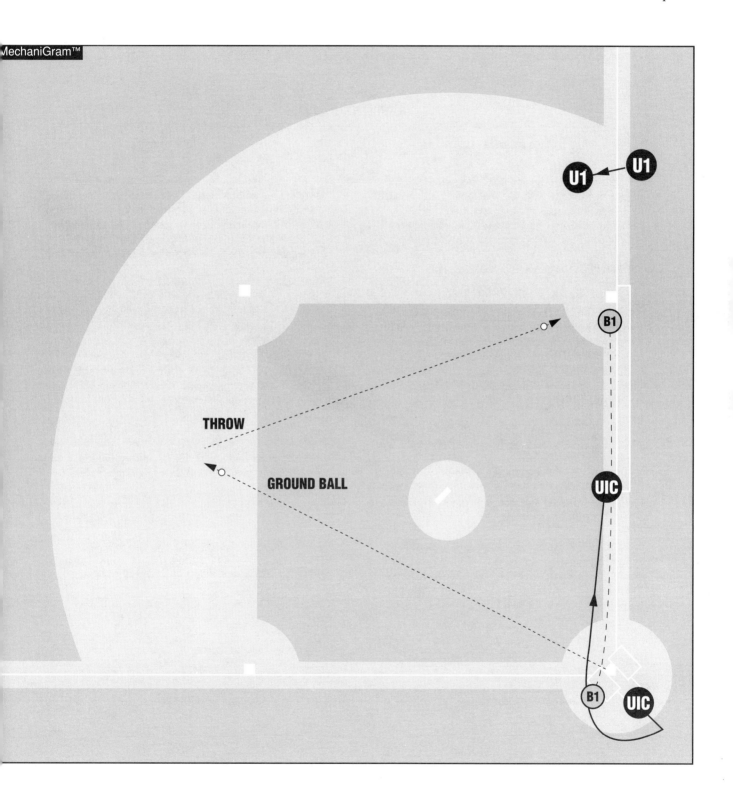

Case Study 6 — Ground ball to the right side

Game situation: Nobody on base

Action on the field: Ground ball fielded by F3, or by F4 moving hard toward the right-field line

RESPONSIBILITIES

Base umpire	Plate umpire
1. Pause, read and react. Read the position of the fielder making the play. If F3 fields the ball, move to foul territory to rule on the play at first base; if F4 fields the ball, gage his "pressure" — whenever possible, move into fair territory to rule on the play.	1. Pause, read and react. Read the developing play. If fair/foul is not a factor, clear the catcher and move out to the catcher's left, then trail B1 toward first. If fair/foul is a factor, clear the catcher and establish a position straddling the first-base line or the first-base line extended, set before the play occurs and rule fair or foul.
2. Establish the best angle possible to the developing play.	
3. If there will be a throw, read the throw. On a good throw, come to your set position and focus on the play at first base. On a bad throw, adjust: Move toward the foul line if the throw is wide toward home plate; move in an arc toward home plate if the throw is wide toward right field; lock in and concentrate on your timing if the throw is high or low.	3. Read the fielder. Whether F3 or F4 makes the play, continue trailing B1 toward first base, strive to reach the 45-foot line and set. If F4 makes a bad throw, prepare for a swipe tag, pulled foot or an overthrow.
4. Observe B1's touch of first and listen for the ball to hit F3's glove. *Timing!* Do not rule B1 out unless you are certain F3 has complete control of the ball. If the play breaks down and you are uncertain of a swipe tag or pulled foot, communicate with UIC *before* you rule B1 safe or out.	4. As the play at first develops, come to a standing set and observe the play. Offer your opinion of a swipe tag or pulled foot only if U1 requests help.
5. If F3 fields the ball and there will be no throw, establish your set position before F3 arrives at the base. Be stationary when the play happens. *Timing!* Do not rule B1 out unless you are certain F3 has complete control of the ball.	

Notes

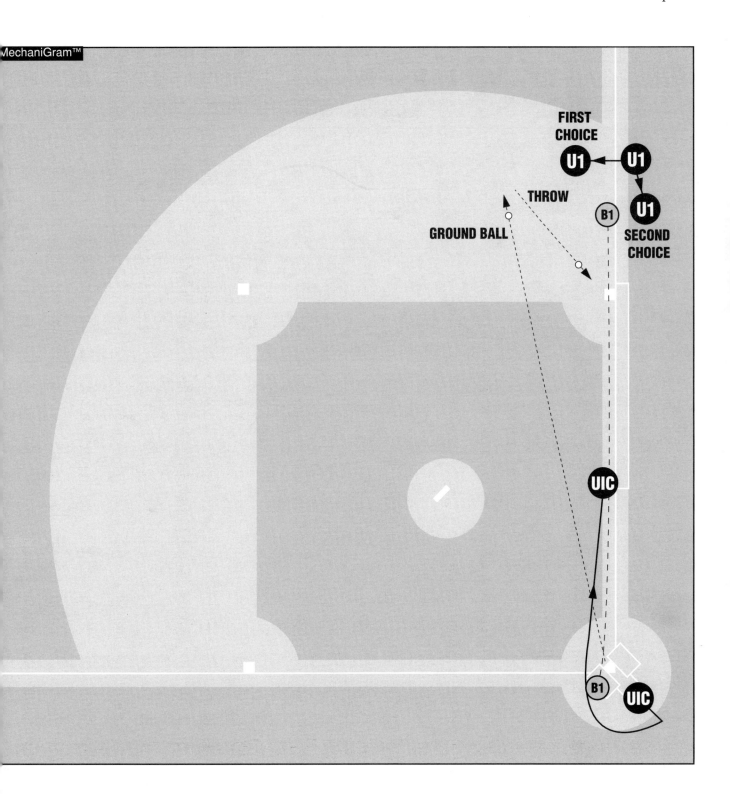

Case Study 7 — Clean hit to the outfield

Game situation: Nobody on base

Action on the field: Clean single to the outfield

RESPONSIBILITIES

Base umpire	Plate umpire
1. Pause, read and react. Read "base hit."	1. Pause, read and react. Read "base hit."
2. Pivot. Be sure to observe B1's touch of first base, then prepare to take B1 to second. *Note: Time your pivot so that your chest is to first base as B1 arrives there.*	2. Read your partner's pivot.
	3. If fair/foul is a consideration: Move aggressively along the foul line, set before the play occurs and rule fair or foul. If fair/foul is not a consideration: Move in a direct line with the flight of the ball, but do not cross an imaginary line between first and third base.
4. Keep your chest to the ball, and glance at B1 to observe his progress. When B1 stops and retreats to first, *always* prepare for a tag play: Keep your chest to the ball and move directly toward the cutout to establish a 90-degree angle between your line of sight and B1's path back to first base.	
	5. Observe the remaining action from a standing set. Your normal responsibilities: an overthrow near a dead-ball area and a play on B1 at home plate.
6. Continue to observe B1 as you move to your position for the next pitch.	

Notes

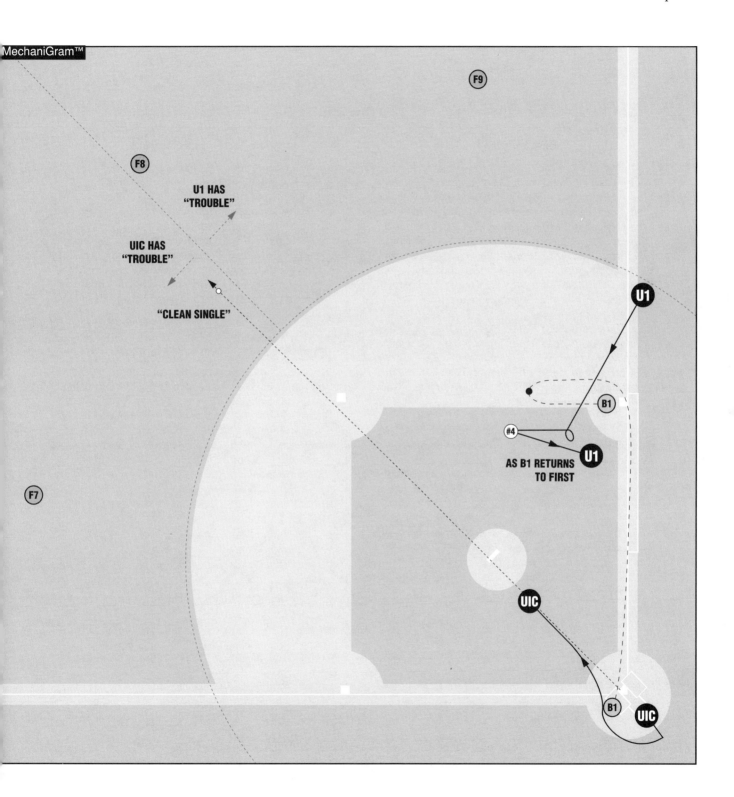

MechaniGram™

F9

F8

U1 HAS
"TROUBLE"

UIC HAS
"TROUBLE"

"CLEAN SINGLE"

F7

U1

B1

#4

U1

AS B1 RETURNS
TO FIRST

UIC

B1

UIC

Case Study 8 — Hit to the outfield, possible extra bases

Game situation: Nobody on base

Action on the field: Batted ball in an outfield gap

RESPONSIBILITIES

Base umpire	Plate umpire
1. Pause, read and react. Read "base hit."	1. Pause, read and react. Read "base hit."
2. Pivot. Be sure to observe B1's touch of first base, then prepare to take B1 to second and to third. *Note: Time your pivot so that your chest is to first base as B1 arrives there.* If it is evident there will not be a play at second base, take an angle behind the mound toward third base. If a play develops at third base, move toward the cutout and make the call.	2. Read your partner's pivot. 3. If fair/foul is a consideration: Move aggressively along the foul line, set before the play occurs and rule fair or foul. If fair/foul is not a consideration: Move in a direct line with the flight of the ball, but do not cross an imaginary line between first and third base.
4. Keep your chest to the ball, and glance at B1 to observe his progress. When B1 rounds first and starts to second, lead him toward second base.	5. As B1 commits to second base, observe the remaining action from a standing set. Your normal responsibilities: an overthrow near a dead-ball area and a play on B1 at home plate. Be prepared to respond and support your partner in case B1 retreats to first base and a rundown develops, or the throw gets away and B1 attempts to advance to third. *Communicate!*
5. Read the outfielder making the play and his throw to second. Establish your set position at the second-base cutout; adjust for the best possible angle as the tag play develops. That is normally a 90-degree angle between your line of sight and B1's path to the base.	
6. *Timing!* Do not rule B1 out unless you are certain the fielder has complete control of the ball.	
7. If B1 is safe, continue to observe B1 as you move to your position for the next pitch.	

Notes

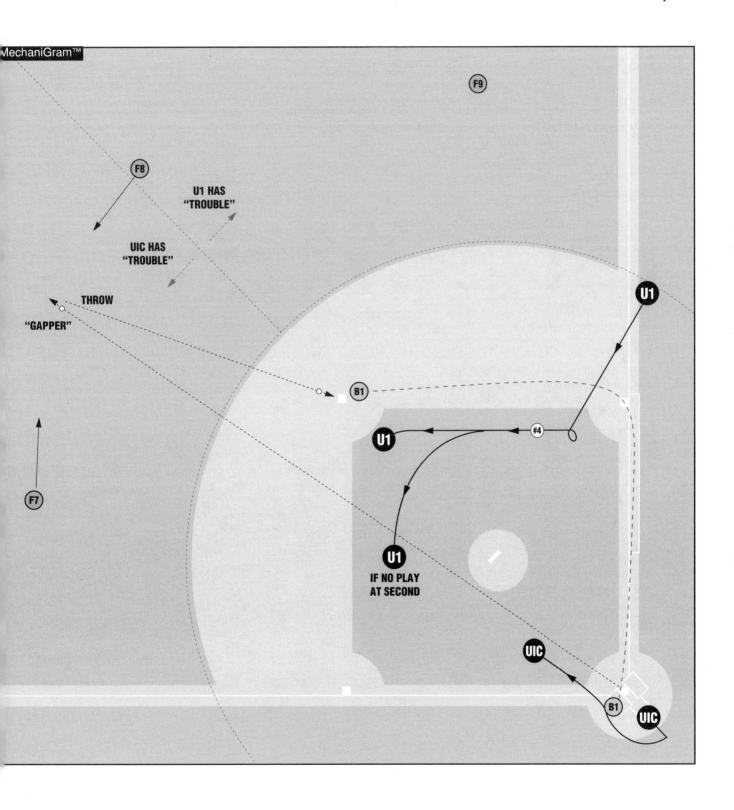

Case Study 9 — Bunt or bouncing ball fielded in "the box"

Game situation: Nobody on base

Action on the field: Batted ball fielded by F1, F2, F3 or F5 in front of home plate

RESPONSIBILITIES

Base umpire	Plate umpire
1. Pause, read and react. Read the batted ball in "the box."	1. Pause, read and react. Read the developing play.
2. Move very quickly to a fair-territory location near the first base cutout, 12 to 15 feet from first base.	
	3. Rule fair or foul as necessary.
4. Establish a position two or three steps off the foul line.	4. Clear the catcher and move out to the catcher's left, then trail B1 toward first.
5. If there will be a throw, read the throw. On a good throw, come to your set position and focus on the play at first base. On a bad throw, adjust: Move toward the foul line if the throw is wide toward home plate; move in an arc toward home plate if the throw is wide toward right field; lock in and concentrate on your timing if the throw is high or low.	5. Read the throw. On a good throw, continue trailing B1 toward first base, strive to reach the 45-foot line and set. On a bad throw, prepare for a collision, swipe tag, pulled foot or an overthrow.
6. Be aware of the potential for running-lane interference by B1, but remember that is *primarily* the plate umpire's call.	6. Be alert for running-lane interference by B1 and rule immediately if interference occurs — that is *primarily* your call.
	7. As the play at first develops, come to a standing set and observe the play. Offer your opinion of a swipe tag or pulled foot only if U1 requests help.
8. Observe B1's touch of first and listen for the ball to hit the fielder's glove.	
9. *Timing!* Do not rule B1 out unless you are certain the fielder has complete control of the ball. If the play breaks down and you are uncertain of a swipe tag or pulled foot, communicate with UIC *before* you rule B1 safe or out.	

Notes

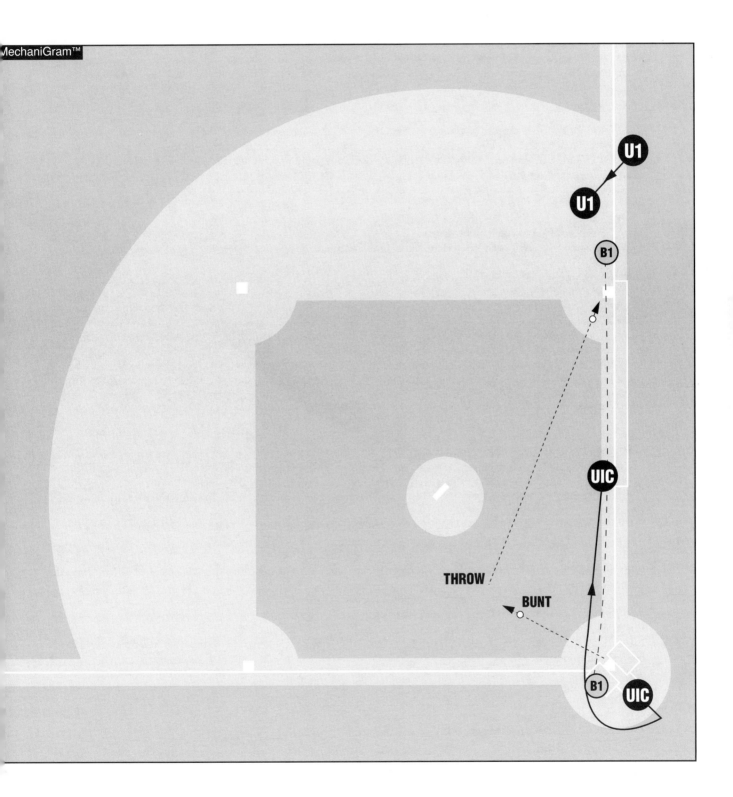

Review: Bases empty

Base umpire
- Start in position A.
- Adjust according to the first baseman's position.
- Fair/foul: You have batted balls on the first-base side that go beyond the base.
- Field coverage: You have batted balls to the outfield beginning with anything hit directly at the center fielder, extending through right field and to the dead-ball area near the right-field line.
- On the bases: If you cover a fly ball, you will attempt to return to cover a play at the plate; if you do not cover a fly ball, you are responsible for the batter-runner at first, second and third base.
- Priorities:
    1. An illegal pitch.
    2. Help for the plate umpire on the half-swing.
    3. Batted ball that travels beyond first base — rule fair or foul at or near the right-field line.
    4. A "trouble ball" in your area of the outfield — beginning with any ball hit directly to F8 and extending to dead-ball territory outside the right-field line.
    5. A ground ball in the infield: You have the play on B1 at first base and any play that develops at first, second and third.
    6. A batted or bunted ball with F3, F1 and B1 all converging at the base.
    7. "Pressure" from the second baseman.
    8. A clean hit, or any batted ball to UIC's area of the outfield.

Umpire in chief
- Your first concern is always the pitch: strike or ball.
- Fair/foul: You have all batted balls on the third-base side, and batted balls on the first-base side which do not physically pass the base.
- Field coverage: You have batted balls to the outfield beginning with anything hit to the center fielder's right, extending through left field and to the dead-ball area near the left-field line.
- On the bases: If you cover a fly ball, you must to return to cover a play at the plate; if you do not cover a fly ball, you are responsible for the batter-runner at first, second and third base, and you have primary responsibility for the batter-runner trying to score (until U1 communicates and takes the play at the plate).
- Priorities:
    1. An illegal pitch.
    2. The pitch: ball or strike.
    3. Check-swings and defensive appeals.
    4. Slow-rolling ball down either base line: fair/foul from home plate to either bag.
    5. A fair/foul call down the third-base or left-field line, or between home plate and first base.
    6. A "trouble" ball in your area of the outfield — beginning with any ball hit to the center fielder's right and extending to the dead-ball area outside the left-field line.
    7. A bunted ball when opponents converge — interference/obstruction.

Quiz

Without referring back, you should be able to answer the following true-false questions. Remember: R1 is always the runner who begins a play at first base; R2 at second; R3 at third; B1 is the batter-runner; fielders are identified by their scoring abbreviations (F1 is the pitcher, F2 the catcher, etc.).

1. When a batted ball in the outfield is not in his area, the base umpire will *always* pivot.
2. When U1 "goes" on a batted ball to the outfield, UIC will clear the catcher and take a path to the first-base side of the mound to trail B1.
3. When F6 fields a ground ball, if the throw to first is wide toward home plate U1 will adjust by moving toward the first-base cutout.
4. During a ground-ball play at first base, UIC will rule B1 guilty of interference only if U1 requests help.
5. If a batted ball bounces 20-feet short of the right-field wall, U1 determines fair/foul.
6. If B1 doubles in the left-field gap, UIC covers a play at third base.

Runner configuration: Runner at first base

Base umpire position: Position B.
  Adjustment factors:
    Game situation: Is a bunt in order? Adjust forward a step or two. When a bunt does occur, it will be easier to move into position and prepare for a play at first base; if the bunt is missed and a pickoff throw goes to first, again it will be easier to move into position. Is the game one-sided? That means conservative base running, few steals and almost no bunting, so you can move back one or two steps from your normal position. That will make it easier to set and adjust when a tag play develops at second base.

    Defensive tendencies: If the pitcher has a good pickoff move, you may want to adjust forward a step or two toward home plate. On a pickoff play, that will open the angle between your line of sight and the runner's return path to first base. You would make the same adjustment, although not by as many steps, if the catcher makes pickoff throws himself.

    The runner: If R1 is a recognized base stealer or if the situation seems "right" for a steal, or if the pitcher has a notoriously bad pickoff move, adjust back from your normal position.

    The batter: Simply for your personal safety, if B1 is an unusually strong, left-handed pull hitter, you might consider adjusting back a step. That will give you more time to react to a ball batted in your direction. You'll rarely be hurt by that step because the kind of power hitter we're discussing rarely has a runner steal in front of him. Coaches don't want to "take the bat out of his hand."

In order of importance, be prepared for the following situations:
    1. A balk or illegal pitch.
    2. Pick off attempt at first base by the pitcher.
    3. Help for the plate umpire on the check-swing.
    4. Pick off attempt at first base by the catcher.
    5. A second-base steal attempt by R1.
    6. A "trouble ball" in your area of the outfield — the "V," beginning with any ball hit directly to F7 and ending with any ball hit directly to F9.
    7. A ground ball in the infield: You have the first play in the infield, both ends of a double play and all plays at second base; UIC has responsibility for a subsequent play at third base and any play that develops at home plate.
    8. A batted or bunted ball with F1, F3, F4 and/or B1 converging at the base.
    9. A ball hit to the outfield followed by a play on R1 advancing to second or retreating to first.
    10. R1 advancing to third or B1 advancing to second on a hit down the right-field line.

Plate umpire anticipation:
Your initial position is always behind the plate. As the pitcher begins his delivery, come set in your stance. Your initial responsibility is always calling the pitch a strike or a ball. Respond to the batted ball and the action as it develops.

    Batted ball in the infield: Determine fair/foul as appropriate. U1 will always rule on the first play in the infield; you have primary responsibility for a subsequent play at third base and for any play at home plate. In the event of a double-play opportunity, move toward third base as you observe the action at second base: If R1 is retired, stop and return to home plate or to a position straddling the first-base line and be prepared to assist (if necessary) with a swipe tag at first base; if R1 is not retired, continue toward third-base and prepare for a subsequent play on R1; cover dead-ball areas in case of an errant throw.

    Batted ball to the outfield: You have the areas from F7 to the left-field dead-ball area and from F9 to the right-field dead-ball area. To right field: Trail B1 toward first base; rule fair/foul and catch/no catch as necessary. To center field or left field: Move into infield and rule fair/foul, catch/no catch as necessary; you are responsible for R1 if he attempts to advance from first to third on any batted ball.

In order of importance, be prepared for the following situations:
    1. A balk or illegal pitch.
    2. The pitch: ball or strike.
    3. Check-swings and defensive appeals.
    4. A fair/foul call down either foul line.
    5. A "trouble" ball in your area of the outfield.
    6. A double-play ball in the infield — observe and support U1.
    7. A bunted ball when opponents converge — interference/obstruction.
    8. R1 advancing from first to third on any batted ball.

Case Study 10 — Pickoff throw to first

Game situation: Runner at first base

Action on the field: Pitcher attempts pickoff at first base

RESPONSIBILITIES

Base umpire	Plate umpire
1. Read the pitcher's move to first base.	1. Read the pitcher's move to first base.
2. Step directly forward toward home plate. Ideally you will step with your right foot, then your left foot, then pivot on your left foot as you take a final step with your right foot and turn to observe the play. (At a minimum, step left, pivot and turn as you step right.) The steps will open your angle to view the play.	2. Observe the pitcher's entire move to insure there is no balk.
3. Set. Observe the play.	3. Step back to obtain a clear view of the play at first base; observe the play.
4. *Timing!* Do not rule B1 out unless you are certain F3 has complete control of the ball. If the play breaks down due to a bad throw, prepare to lead R1 to second base.	5. Read the throw. If the throw is errant, move toward the ball and rule on an overthrow near a dead-ball area.
6. If he is not retired, continue to observe R1 as long as F3 has the ball.	

Notes

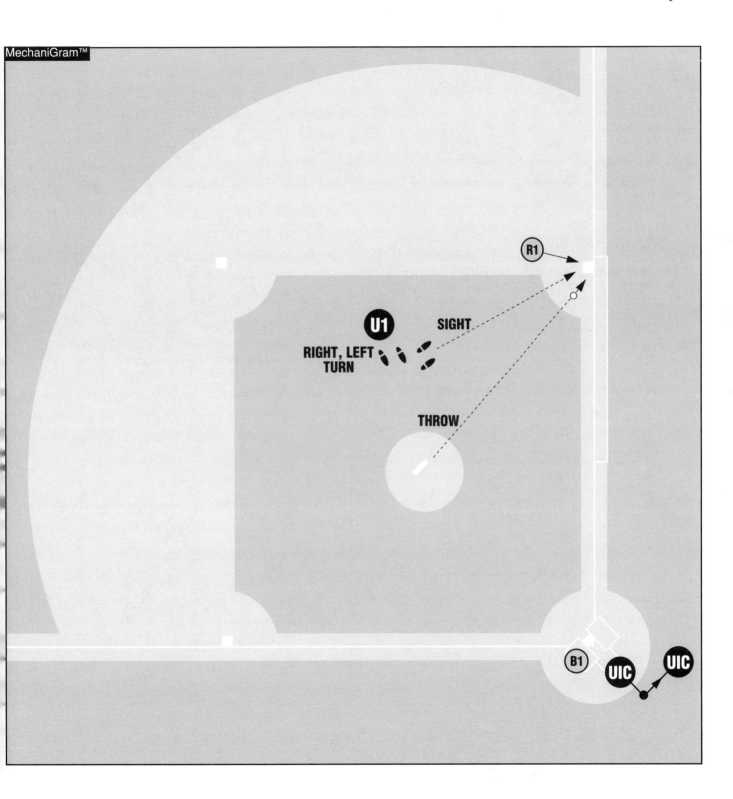

Case Study 11 — Second-base steal

Game situation: Runner at first base

Action on the field: R1 is stealing

RESPONSIBILITIES

Base umpire	Plate umpire
1. Read the runner's break in your peripheral vision.	1. Call the pitch: ball or strike.
	2. Observe the action at home plate — is B1 guilty of interfering with F2's throw?
3. Keep your chest to the ball as you turn your shoulders slightly to your right and take several cross-over steps toward second. Move toward, but not into the cutout.	
4. Read the throw and prepare to adjust on a bad throw.	5. Read the throw. If the throw is errant, prepare to move toward the dead-ball area on the third-base side. If a play at third develops, rule on an overthrow near a dead-ball area.\
5. Let the throw turn you toward second base ("open the gate"). If the throw is wide toward left field, move closer to second base; on any other bad throw, adjust by moving closer to the direct line between first and second.	
6. Set. Observe the play. *Timing!* Do not rule R1 out unless you are certain the fielder has complete control of the ball. If the play breaks down due to a bad throw, prepare to lead R1 to third base.	
7. If he is not retired, continue to observe R1 as long as the fielder has the ball.	

Notes

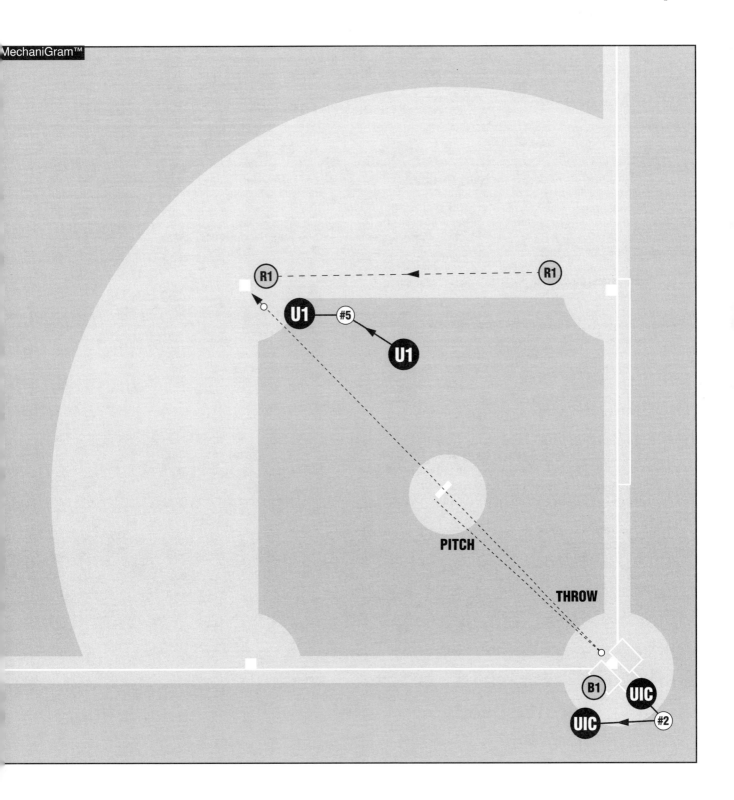

Case Study 12 — Routine fly ball in the "V"

Game situation: Runner at first base

Action on the field: B1 flies to the middle of the outfield

RESPONSIBILITIES

Base umpire

1. Step up, turn and face the ball; pause, read and react. Read the position of the fielder making the play and determine whether this is a ball in your coverage area (it is) and whether this is a "trouble" ball (it is not).

2. Since it is not a "trouble" ball: Move back two or three steps toward the pitcher's mound to "open" your field of view.

3. If there is a catch (there is), signal only if the catch is made "below the knee"; verbally inform your partner of a routine catch. If a difficult play results in no catch, signal "safe" and verbally call, "No catch! No catch!"

4. After the catch: You have tag-up responsibility at first base. If R1 is "half way," move toward the cutout as you read the throw to the infield. If necessary, move into position for a developing play. If R1 is tagging to advance, move toward the second-base cutout as you read the throw to second. Establish your set position before the play occurs. *Timing!*

5. If R1 remains on base, observe R1 whenever the ball is near his location.

Plate umpire

1. Pause, read and react. Read the developing play and your partner.

2. With the ball in U1's coverage area, move 15 to 20 feet up the third-base line in foul territory to observe the play.

Notes

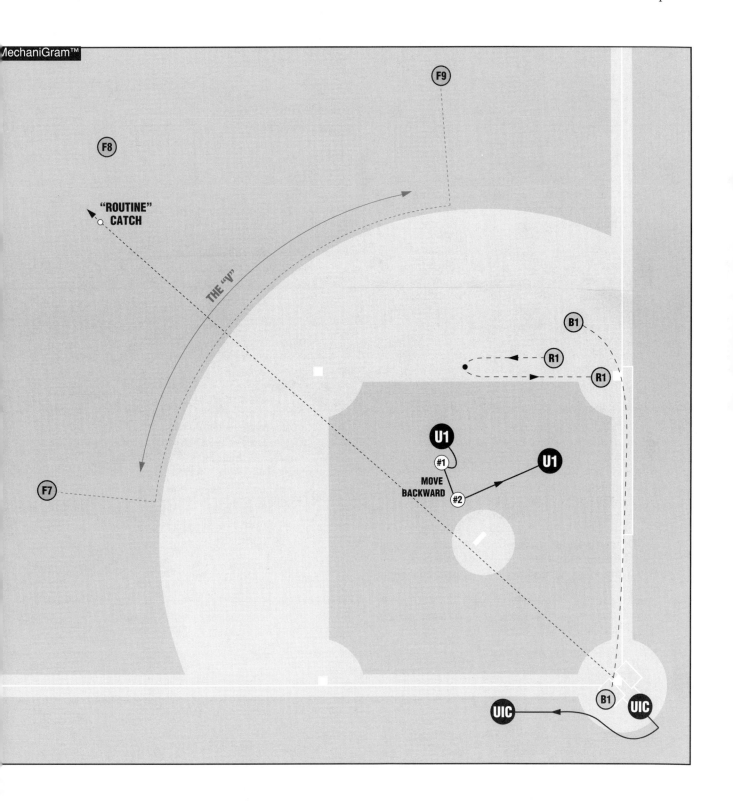

Case Study 13 — Routine fly ball down the left-field line

Game situation: Runner at first base

Action on the field: Left fielder moves toward the line on a fly ball

RESPONSIBILITIES

Base umpire	Plate umpire
1. Step up, turn and face the ball; pause, read and react. Read the position of the fielder making the play and determine whether this is a ball in your coverage area (it is not).	1. Pause, read and react. Read the position of the fielder making the play and determine whether this is a ball in your coverage area (it is) and whether this is a "trouble" ball (it is not).
2. Since the ball is not in your area: Move back two or three steps toward the pitcher's mound to "open" your field of view. Remain aware of the fly ball status as you observe both R1 and B1; insure the batter-runner does not pass his teammate. Listen for your partner to inform you of a catch.	2. Since the ball is in your coverage area, clear the catcher and move about half way up the third-base line; communicate with your partner: "I've got the ball!"
	3. If fair/foul is a consideration, move aggressively along the third-base line, set before the play occurs and rule fair or foul.
	4. Develop the best angle possible to observe the catch/no catch.
	5. If there is a catch (there is), signal only if the catch is made "below the knee"; verbally inform your partner: "Bill, that's a catch." If the ball is a hit, you are responsible for R1 advancing to third base.
6. After the catch: You have tag-up responsibility at first base. If R1 is "half way," move toward the cutout as you read the throw to the infield. If necessary, move into position for a developing play. If R1 is tagging to advance, move toward the second-base cutout as you read the throw to second. Establish your set position before the play occurs. *Timing!*	
7. If R1 remains on base, observe R1 whenever the ball is near his location.	

Notes

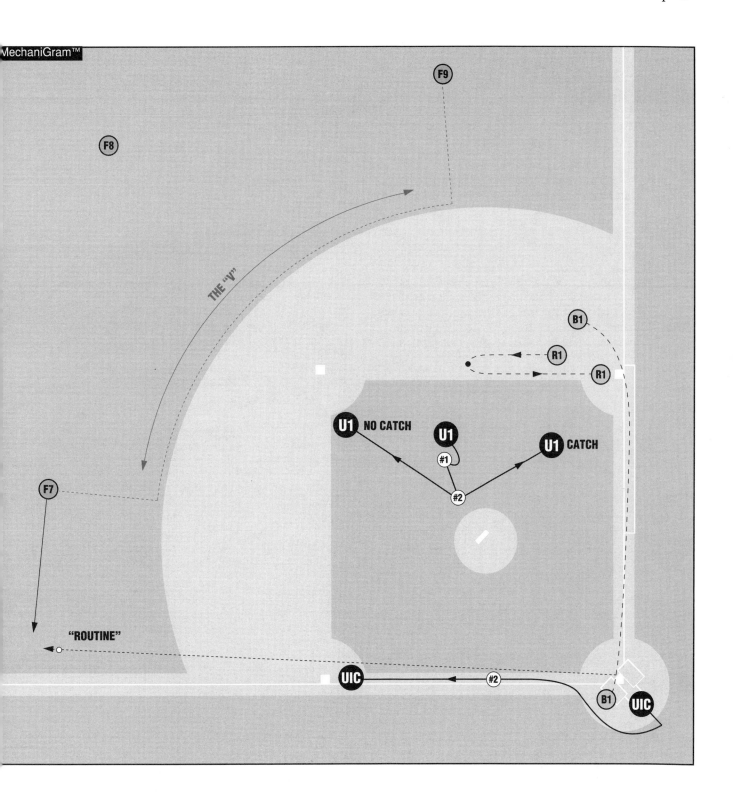

Case Study 14 — Routine fly ball down the right-field line

Game situation: Runner at first base

Action on the field: Right fielder moves toward the line on a fly ball

RESPONSIBILITIES

Base umpire	Plate umpire
1. Step up, turn and face the ball; pause, read and react. Read the position of the fielder making the play and determine whether this is a ball in your coverage area (it is not).	1. Pause, read and react. Read the position of the fielder making the play and determine whether this is a ball in your coverage area (it is) and whether this is a "trouble" ball (it is not).
2. Since the ball is not in your area: Move back two or three steps toward the pitcher's mound to "open" your field of view; because your partner is on the line, prepare to take R1 into third base if the ball is not caught. Remain aware of the fly ball status as you observe both R1 and B1; insure the batter-runner does not pass his teammate. Listen for your partner to inform you of a catch.	2. Since the ball is in your coverage area, clear the catcher and move about half way up the first-base line; communicate with your partner: "I'm on the line!"
	3. If fair/foul is a consideration, move aggressively along the first-base line, set before the play occurs and rule fair or foul.
	4. Develop the best angle possible to observe the catch/no catch.
	5. If there is a catch (there is), signal only if the catch is made "below the knee"; verbally inform your partner: "Bill, that's a catch." If the ball is a hit, you are responsible for out-of-play areas and for any play that develops at home plate.
7. If R1 is tagging to advance, move toward the second-base cutout as you read the throw to second. Establish your set position before the play occurs. *Timing!*	6. After the catch: You have tag-up responsibility at first base. If R1 is "half way," move toward the cutout as you read the throw to the infield. If necessary, move into position for a developing play.
8. If R1 remains on base, observe R1 whenever the ball is near his location.	

Notes

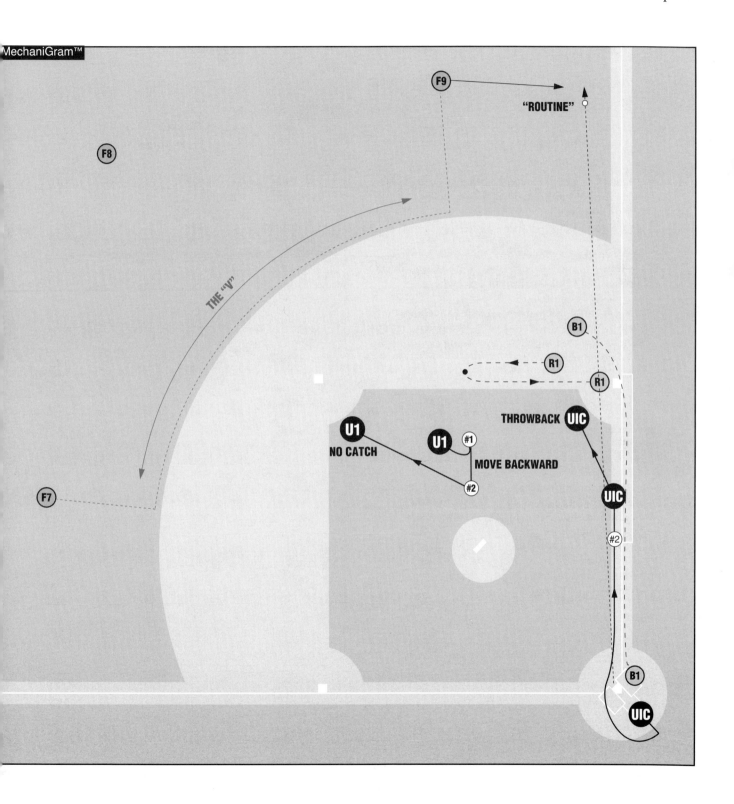

Case Study 15 — "Trouble" ball in the "V"

Game situation: Runner at first base

Action on the field: B1 flies to the middle of the outfield — "trouble" ball

RESPONSIBILITIES

Base umpire	Plate umpire
1. Step up, turn and face the ball; pause, read and react. Read the position of the fielder making the play and determine whether this is a ball in your coverage area (it is) and whether this is a "trouble" ball (it is).	1. Pause, read and react. Read the developing play and your partner.
2. Since it is a "trouble" ball: Move to the edge of the infield grass in the direction of the ball to rule on the play. _Do not leave the infield grass!_	2. Because this is a "trouble" ball, a developing play at third base is likely. Move at least half way up the third-base line in foul territory and prepare to cover a play.
3. If there is a catch (there is), signal only if the catch is made "below the knee"; verbally inform your partner of a routine catch. If a difficult play results in no catch, signal "safe" and verbally call, "No catch! No catch!"	
4. After the catch: You have tag-up responsibility at first base. If R1 is "half way," move aggressively toward the cutout as you read the throw to the infield. If necessary, move into position for a developing play. If R1 is tagging to advance: First, move two or three steps back toward the pitcher's mound to open your field of view; read the throw; as a play develops, move toward the second-base cutout. Establish your set position before the play occurs. _Timing!_	
5. If R1 remains on base, observe R1 whenever the ball is near his location.	

Notes

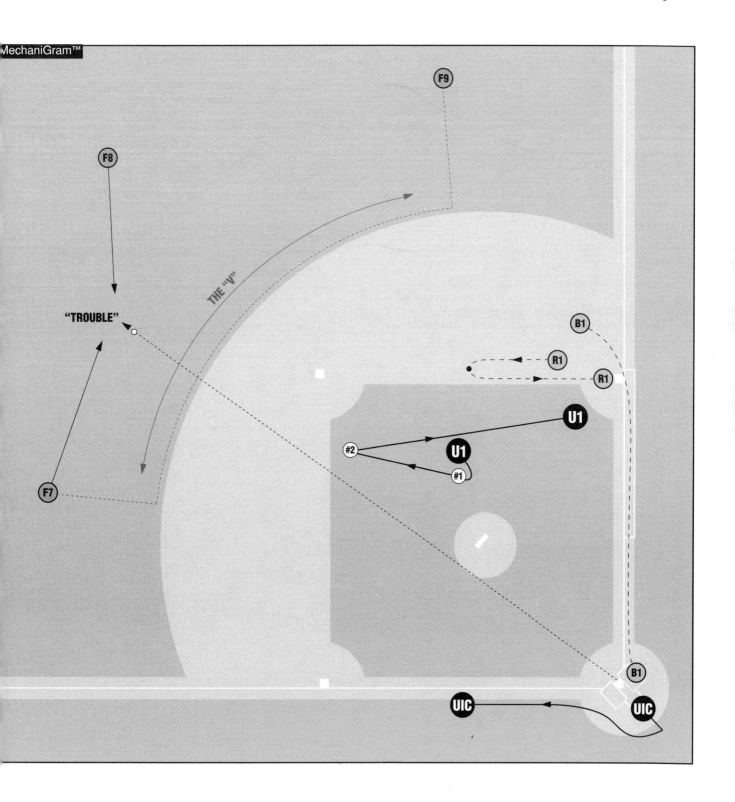

Case Study 16 — "Trouble" ball down the left-field line

Game situation: Runner at first base

Action on the field: Left fielder moves toward the line on a "trouble" ball

RESPONSIBILITIES

Base umpire

1. Step up, turn and face the ball; pause, read and react. Read the position of the fielder making the play and determine whether this is a ball in your coverage area (it is not).

2. Since the ball is not in your area: Move back two or three steps toward the pitcher's mound to "open" your field of view. Remain aware of the fly ball status as you observe both R1 and B1; insure the batter-runner does not pass his teammate. Listen for your partner to inform you of a catch.

6. After the catch: You have tag-up responsibility at first base. If R1 is "half way," move toward the cutout as you read the throw to the infield. If necessary, move into position for a developing play. If R1 is tagging to advance, move toward the second-base cutout as you read the throw to second. Establish your set position before the play occurs. *Timing!*

7. If R1 remains on base, observe R1 whenever the ball is near his location.

Plate umpire

1. Pause, read and react. Read the position of the fielder making the play and determine whether this is a ball in your coverage area (it is) and whether this is a "trouble" ball (it is).

2. Since this is a "trouble" ball in your coverage area, clear the catcher and move as far toward the play as possible to rule on the play as you communicate with your partner: "I've got the ball!"

3. If fair/foul is a consideration, remain along the third-base line. Set before the play occurs and rule fair or foul.

4. Develop the best angle possible to observe the catch/no catch.

5. If there is a catch (there is), signal only if the catch is made "below the knee"; verbally inform your partner: "Bill, that's a catch." If the ball is a hit, you are responsible for R1 advancing to third base.

Notes

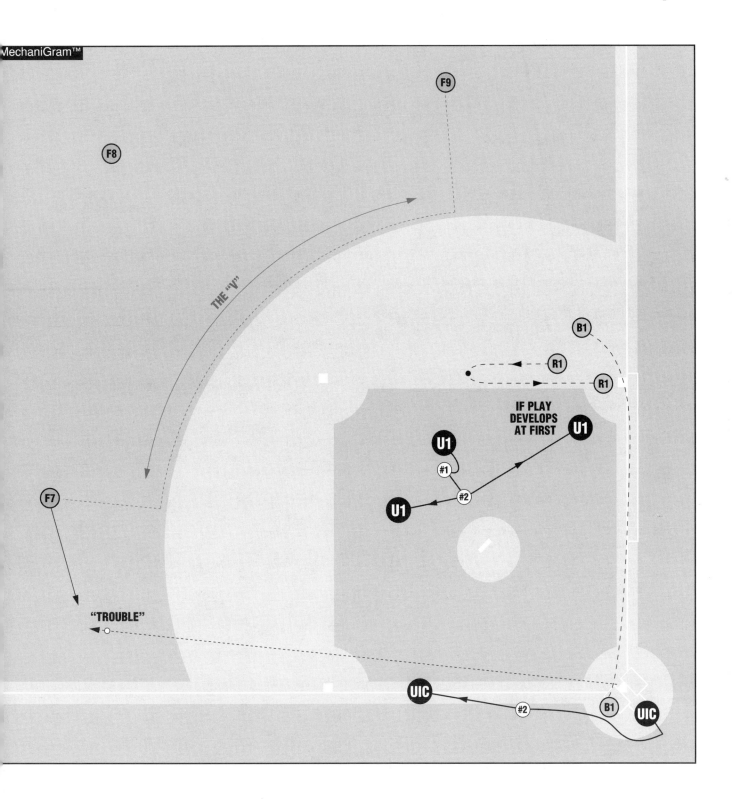

Case Study 17 — "Trouble" ball down the right-field line: no catch

Game situation: Runner at first base

Action on the field: Right fielder moves toward the line on a "trouble" ball

RESPONSIBILITIES

Base umpire	Plate umpire
1. Step up, turn and face the ball; pause, read and react. Read the position of the fielder making the play and determine whether this is a ball in your coverage area (it is not).	1. Pause, read and react. Read the position of the fielder making the play and determine whether this is a ball in your coverage area (it is) and whether this is a "trouble" ball (it is).
2. Since the ball is not in your area: Move back two or three steps toward the pitcher's mound to "open" your field of view; because your partner is on the line, prepare to take R1 into third base if the ball is not caught. Remain aware of the fly ball status as you observe both R1 and B1; insure the batter-runner does not pass his teammate. Listen for your partner to inform you of a catch.	2. Since this is a "trouble" ball in your coverage area, clear the catcher and move as far toward the play as possible to rule on the play as you communicate with your partner: "I'm on the line!"
	3. If fair/foul is a consideration, move aggressively along the first-base line, set before the play occurs and rule fair or foul.
	4. Develop the best angle possible to observe the catch/no catch.
	5. If there is a catch (there is not), signal no catch. If the ball is a hit, you are responsible for out-of-play areas and for any play that develops at home plate.
6. If there is no catch, read R1's advancement. If it appears R1 will advance toward third base, move toward the shortstop position.	
7. Read the throw from the outfielder or cutoff man and move into the developing play at second base or third base.	

Notes

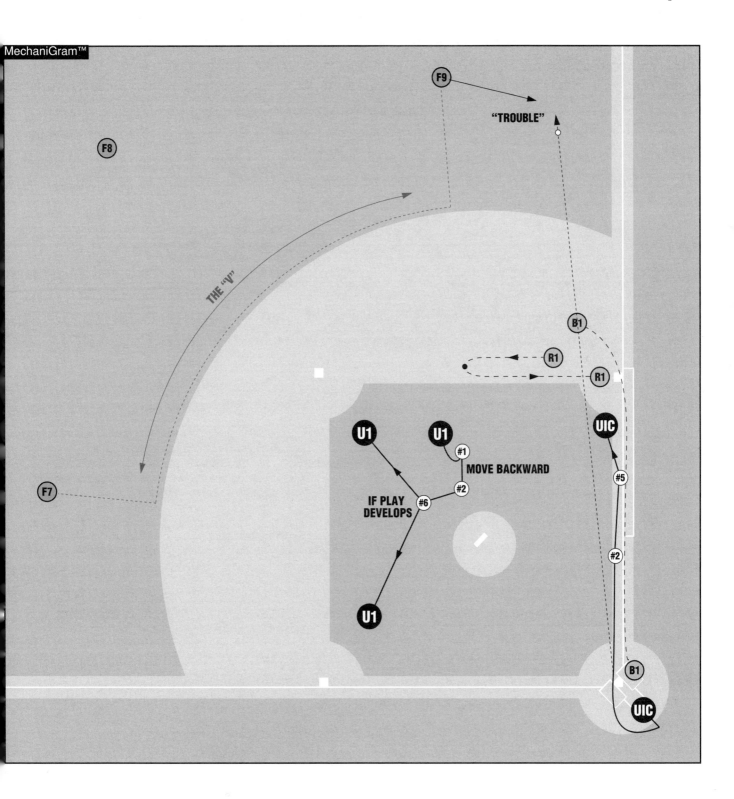

MechaniGram™

F9

"TROUBLE"

F8

THE "V"

B1

R1

R1

UIC

F7

U1   U1   #1

MOVE BACKWARD

#5

#2   #2

IF PLAY
DEVELOPS   #6

U1

B1

UIC

Case Study 18 — Ground ball to the infield

Game situation: Runner at first base

Action on the field: B1 hits ground ball played in the infield

RESPONSIBILITIES

Base umpire

1. Step up, turn and face the ball; read ground ball and possible double play.

3. If the batted ball is mishandled, prepare for the first play at either second or first base. If the batted ball is fielded cleanly (it is), prepare for a double-play attempt.

4. Let the infielder's throw to second base turn your shoulders square to the bag. *Determine* safe/out of R1. (*Timing!* Do not rule R1 out unless the fielder has complete control of the ball.)

5. Turn slightly (chest to right field or the right field corner); observe the remaining action at second base as you move toward the first base line (as far as the play will allow, usually two or three steps) and prepare for the relay to first. *Declare* R1 out or safe, aloud, *while moving* toward the first base line.

6. Let the relay throw turn you toward first base. (The play at first will happen very quickly, so be prepared.)

7. Set for play at first and observe the play. *Timing!* Do not rule B1 out unless the fielder has complete control of the ball.

8. When the play is over, if either runner remains on base, observe the runner whenever the ball is near his location.

NOTE: Proper timing on the turn to first will keep your eyes on the ball until the fielder makes the relay throw. If the play breaks down (dropped ball, errant throw, interference at second) move directly to second base and "sell" your out or safe decision with an emphatic voice-and-signal combination.

Plate umpire

1. Pause, read and react. Read the possible double-play ball.

2. Clear the catcher; if the ball is hit near the first-base line, you must first rule fair or foul. Move toward second base to the third base side of the pitcher's mound. *If R1 advances to third, you have the play.*

5. Go as far as you can until your partner calls out R1 (he does).

6. Stop, turn and move into position to observe the subsequent play at first base and support your partner. Be prepared to rule on interference by B1 or an overthrow; offer your opinion of a swipe tag or pulled foot only if U1 requests help.

NOTE: If R1 is safe at second, do not return to the plate area. A play at third base is your responsibility.

Notes

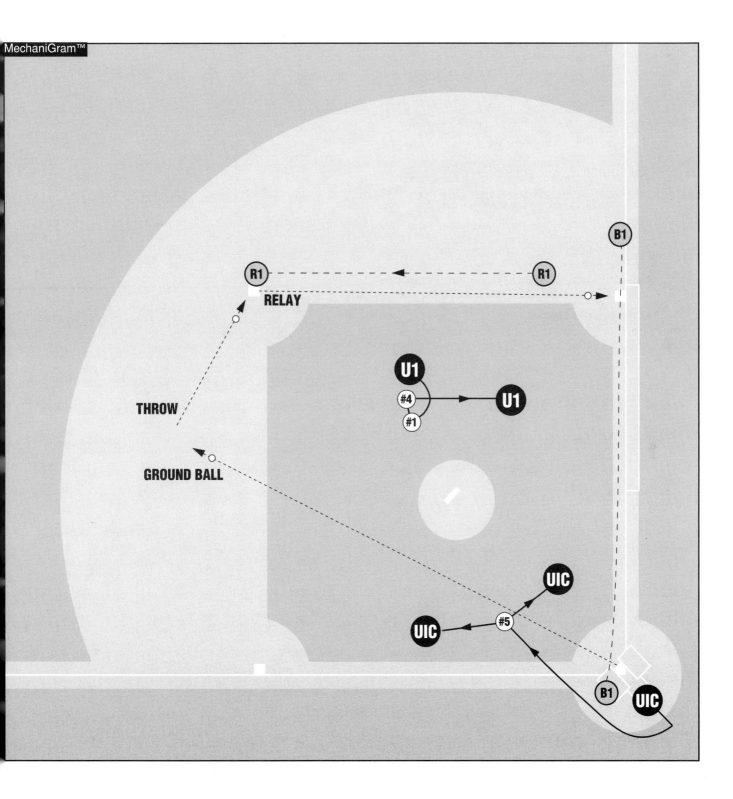

Case Study 19 — Ground ball to the first baseman

Game situation: Runner at first base

Action on the field: B1 hits ground ball or bouncing ball to F3 to start a "reverse double play"

RESPONSIBILITIES

Base umpire	Plate umpire
1. Step up, turn and face the ball; read ground ball and probable first play at first base. (For a first play at second base, see Case Play #18.)	1. Pause, read and react. Read the batted ball near the line and a possible double-play ball.
	2. Clear the catcher and move up the first-base line; rule fair/foul as appropriate.
3. If the batted ball is fielded cleanly (it is), prepare for a double-play attempt. Turn chest to the base and rule B1 out or safe. *Timing!* Do not rule B1 out unless the fielder has complete control of the ball.	
	4. Come to a standing set and observe the play at first base. Be prepared to rule on interference by B1 or an overthrow.
5. If a subsequent play develops, turn and move toward the second-base cutout. Let F3's throw turn you to the play; establish your set position and observe the *tag play*. (*Timing!* Do not rule R1 out unless the fielder has complete control of the ball.)	5. When the play at first base is complete, move into fair territory and observe subsequent action.
6. If the play breaks down in any manner, you are responsible for plays at first, second *and third* (UIC is "on the line" and cannot move all the way across the diamond).	

Notes

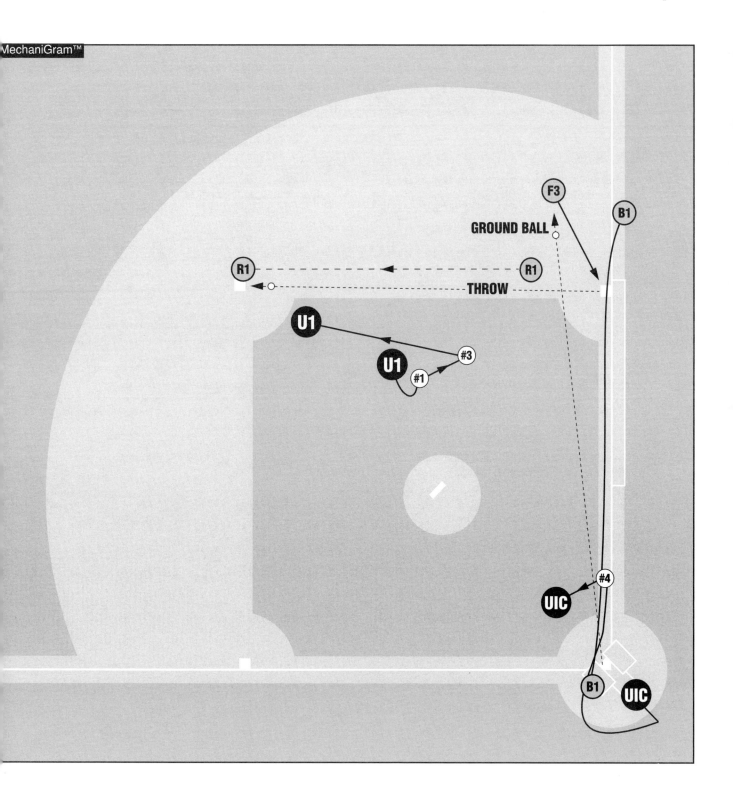

Case Study 20 — Base hit to left field

Game situation: Runner at first base

Action on the field: Clean hit to left field

RESPONSIBILITIES

Base umpire	Plate umpire
1. Step up, turn and face the ball; pause, read and react. Read the position of the fielder making the play and determine whether this is a ball in your coverage area (it is not).	1. Pause, read and react. Read the position of the fielder making the play and determine whether this is a ball in your coverage area (it is) and whether this is a "trouble" ball (it is not).
2. Since the ball is not in your area: Move back two or three steps toward the pitcher's mound to "open" your field of view. Remain aware of the status of the ball as you observe both R1 and B1 advancing to touch bases.	2. Clear the catcher and remain in foul territory as you move about half way up the third-base line. If R1 advances to third, communicate with your partner: "Bill, I've got third! I've got third!"
	3. If fair/foul is a consideration, move aggressively along the third-base line, set before the play occurs and rule fair or foul.
	4. Maintain careful observation of the play on the ball; glance at R1 as he approaches second base. If R1 advances to third, you are responsible for any play that develops at third or home.
5. As the ball returns to the infield, you are responsible for any play that develops at first or second base.	
6. When both runners remain on base, observe R1 and B1 whenever the ball is near either runner's location.	
	6. When both runners remain on base, insure your partner is observing the action before you return to your position at home plate.

Notes

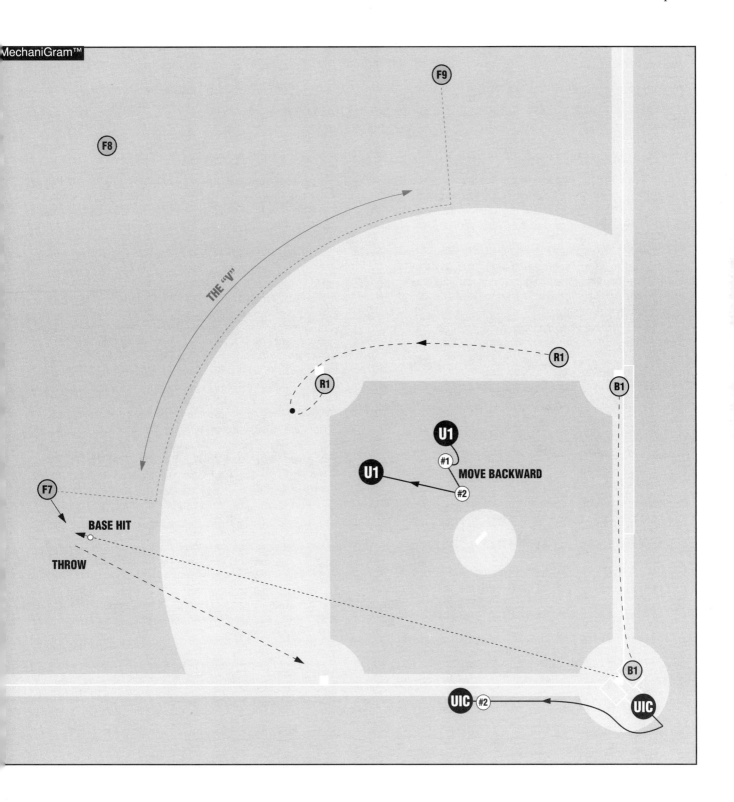

Case Study 21 — Base hit to right field

Game situation: Runner at first base

Action on the field: Clean hit to right field; R1 advances to third

RESPONSIBILITIES

Base umpire	Plate umpire
1. Step up, turn and face the ball; pause, read and react. Read the position of the fielder making the play and determine whether this is a ball in your coverage area (it is not).	1. Pause, read and react. Read the position of the fielder making the play and determine whether this is a ball in your coverage area (it is) and whether this is a "trouble" ball (it is not).
2. Since the ball is not in your area: Move back two or three steps toward the pitcher's mound to "open" your field of view. Remain aware of the status of the ball as you observe both R1 and B1 advancing to touch bases.	2. Clear the catcher.
3. Anticipate that you may have to take R1 into third base (your partner should tell you what he is doing). If your partner indicates he is covering third, release R1 to your partner when R1 commits to third base.	3. If fair/foul is a consideration, communicate with your partner: "I'm on the line!" Move aggressively along the first-base line, set before the play occurs and rule fair or foul. If fair/foul is not a consideration (it is not), remain in foul territory as you move about half way up the third-base line. If R1 advances to third, communicate with your partner: "I've got third if he comes!"
	4. When R1 commits to third, read the throw from the outfield. If no play develops, remain in foul ground prepared to take R1 to the plate if he attempts to advance. If a play develops (it does) communicate *again* with your partner: "Bill, I'm at third! I'm at third!" Move into fair territory near the third-base cutout and establish your set position before the play occurs.
5. After your partner tells you he is covering third, you are responsible for any play at second base and for any play that develops on B1.	
	6. *Timing!* Do not rule the runner out unless you are certain the fielder has complete control of the ball.
	7. If the play breaks down, you are responsible for any play that develops on the lead runner, including a play at the plate.
9. When your partner clears the runner, you are responsible for any play that occurs on R1 or B1. Observe R1 and B1 whenever the ball is near either runner's location.	8. When the play is over and R1 remains on third, clear the runner before you return to your position at home plate.

Notes

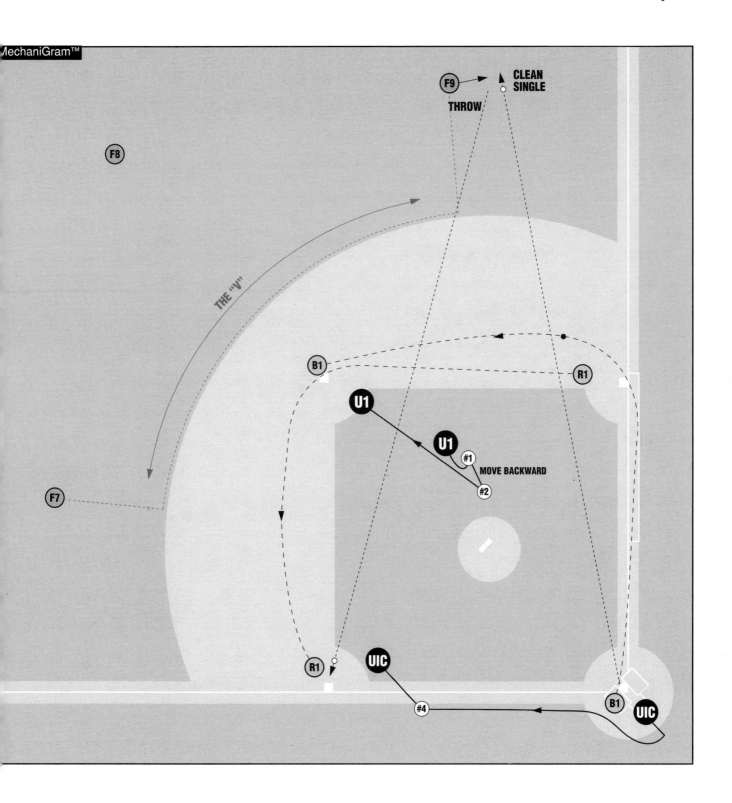

Case Study 22 — Bunt

Game situation: Runner at first base

Action on the field: B1 bunts

RESPONSIBILITIES

Base umpire	Plate umpire
1. Pause, read and react. Read the bunted ball, usually in "the box."	1. Pause, read and react. Read the bunted ball, usually in "the box."
	2. Rule fair or foul as necessary.
3. Read whether the play will develop at first or second base.	
4. Move to establish a 90-degree angle to the expected throw.	4. Clear the catcher and move out to the catcher's left.
5. Read the throw. On a good throw, come to your set position and focus on the play. On a bad throw, adjust to a position which will afford the best possible view of the play: For a play at first base, you'll move closer to the first-base line; for a play at second base, you'll move near the cutout.	5. Read whether the play will develop at first or second base.

6. On a play at first base, observe the action and rule immediately if there is interference by B1. *Prepare to cover third base in the event of a subsequent play.* |
| 7. *Timing!* Do not rule the runner out unless you are certain the fielder has complete control of the ball. If the play breaks down and you are uncertain of a tag or pulled foot, decide whether your partner may be able to assist; if the play is at first base, communicate with UIC *before* you rule B1 safe or out. | 8. Offer your opinion of a swipe tag or pulled foot at first base only if U1 requests help. |
| 9. No matter where the first play develops, recognize the possibility of a subsequent play. | |

Notes

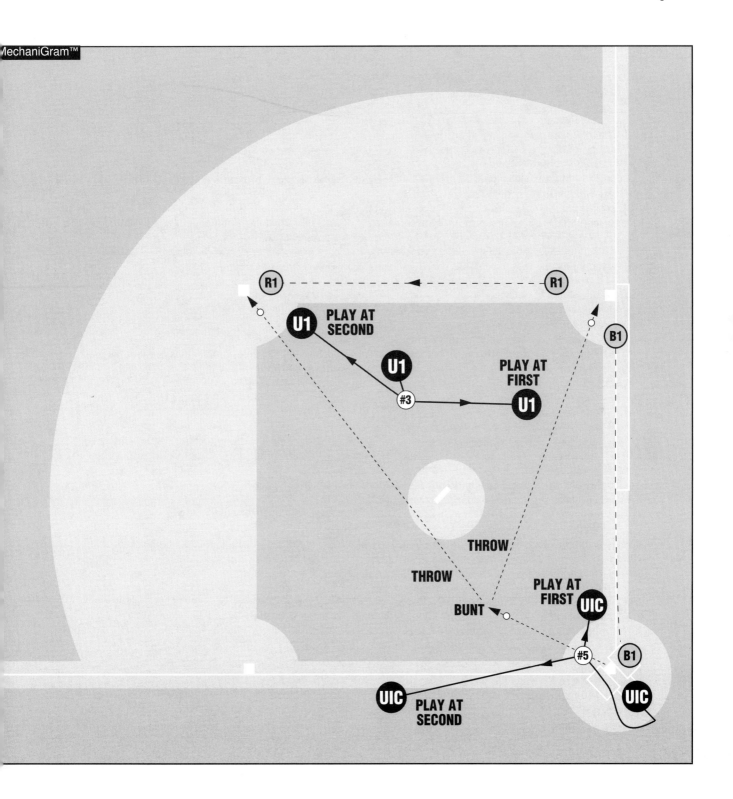

Review: Runner at first base

Base umpire
• Start in position B.
• Adjust according to the game situation, the pitcher's pickoff move and the runner's base-stealing ability.
• Fair/foul: You have no responsibility.
• Field coverage: You have the "V," beginning with any ball hit directly to F7 and ending with any ball hit directly to F9.
• On the bases: You have all plays at first and second, and all plays on B1 at third base.
• Priorities:
    1. A balk or illegal pitch.
    2. Pick off attempt at first base by the pitcher.
    3. Help for the plate umpire on the half-swing.
    4. Pickoff attempt at first base by the catcher.
    5. A second-base steal attempt by R1.
    6. A "trouble ball" in your area of the outfield — the "V," beginning with any ball hit directly to F7 and ending with any ball hit directly to F9.
    7. A ground ball in the infield: You have the first play in the infield, both ends of a double play and all plays at second base; UIC has responsibility for a subsequent play at third base and any play that develops at home plate.
    8. A batted or bunted ball with F1, F3, F4 and/or B1 converging at the base.
    9. A ball hit to left field followed by a play on R1 advancing to second or retreating to first.
    10. R1 advancing to third or B1 advancing to second on a hit down the right-field line.

Umpire in chief
• Your first concern is always the pitch: strike or ball.
• Fair/foul: You have all fair/foul decisions.
• Field coverage: You have balls hit to the outfield to the left or right of the "V."
• On the bases: You have a play on R1 advancing to third on a batted ball (unless a fair/foul or catch/no catch decision requires you to be on the first-base line); you have all plays at home plate.
• Priorities:
    1. A balk or illegal pitch.
    2. The pitch: ball or strike.
    3. Check-swings and defensive appeals.
    4. A fair/foul call down either foul line.
    5. A "trouble" ball in your area of the outfield.
    6. A double-play ball in the infield — observe and support U1.
    7. A bunted ball when opponents converge — interference/obstruction.
    8. R1 advancing from first to third on any batted ball.

Quiz
Without referring back, you should be able to answer the following true-false questions. Remember: R1 is always the runner who begins a play at first base; R2 at second; R3 at third; B1 is the batter-runner; fielders are identified by their scoring abbreviations (F1 is the pitcher, F2 the catcher, etc.).

1. If the pitcher attempts a pickoff throw, U1 steps directly toward the first-base cutout.
2. If B1 singles to right-center field, UIC has the play on R1 advancing to third.
3. If B1 bunts, UIC *may* make the out/safe call on a throw to first base.
4. On a "trouble" ball in the "V," U1 will go to the edge of the outfield grass to observe the catch/no catch.
5. If B1 singles and UIC takes the play on R1 at third, U1 covers home in case of an overthrow.
6. Since U1 has to cover a second-base steal, UIC will observe the action at home plate to rule on interference by B1.

Runner configuration: Runners at first and second

Base umpire position: Position C.

Frequently, in position C you will obstruct the runner's or shortstop's view of the pitcher or the plate. Before a player asks you to move, decide whether you are going to move (you normally should) and in what direction. Also, realize that moving forward or back a step alters your position in the player's view. Even if someone asks you to move "right," you might be better off moving slightly left and a half-step forward or back.

Adjustment factors: (New umpires should work in the basic position. If you have at least three years of field experience, consider the following points and determine whether you want to adjust from your basic position.)

Game situation: Is a bunt in order? Adjust forward a step or two. If a bunt does occur, it will be easier to move into position and prepare for a play at any base; if the bunt is missed and a pickoff throw goes to first, again it will be easier to move into position. Is the game one-sided? That means conservative base running, few steals and almost no bunting, so you can move back one or two steps from your normal position. That will make it easier to set and adjust if a tag play develops at second base.

Defensive tendencies: A pickoff throw to first by the pitcher is unlikely, although not impossible. However, many aggressive catchers like to throw behind the runner at first. If the defense has a reputation for unusual plays or the catcher is unusually aggressive, you may adjust forward a step or two. If the defense has a reputation for second-base pickoffs, you may adjust back a step or two and move a step or two closer to the center of the infield. That will give you more time to set and a better angle for a pickoff play at second.

The runner: If the catcher is at least average for the level of play, third base steals are rare (almost unheard of with no outs or two outs). You may adjust back a step or two. But if R2 is a recognized base stealer or if the situation seems "right" for a steal, adjust forward from your normal position.

The batter: Simply for your personal safety, if B1 is a strong, right-handed pull hitter, you might consider adjusting back a step. That will give you more time to react to a ball batted in your direction. You'll rarely be hurt by that step because the kind of power hitter we're discussing rarely has a runner steal in front of him. Coaches don't want to "take the bat out of his hand."

In order of importance, be prepared for the following situations:
1. A balk or illegal pitch.
2. Pick off attempt at second base by the pitcher.
3. Pick off attempt at first base by the pitcher.
4. Help for the plate umpire on the check-swing.
5. A third-base steal — as F1 delivers, glance over your right shoulder to see if R2 is breaking for third.
6. A double-steal and an unexpected first play at second base.
7. Pick off attempt at first base by the catcher.
8. Pickoff attempt at second base by the catcher.
9. A "trouble ball" in your area of the outfield — the "V," beginning with any ball hit directly to F7 and ending with any ball hit directly to F9.
10. A ground ball in the infield: You have all plays at first, second and third; UIC will "stay home" to observe R2 touching third and will cover all plays at the plate.
11. A batted or bunted ball with F1, F3, F4 and/or B1 converging at the base.
12. A ball hit to the outfield followed by a play on B1 or R1 at any base.
13. An infield fly.

Plate umpire anticipation:
Your initial position is always behind the plate. As the pitcher begins his delivery, come set in your stance. Your initial responsibility is always calling the pitch a strike or a ball. Respond to the batted ball and the action as it develops.

Batted ball in the infield: Determine fair/foul as appropriate. U1 will always rule on the first play in the infield; and for any play that is not at home plate. In the event of a double-play opportunity, observe the action at second base and be prepared to assist (if necessary) with a swipe tag at first base or an ensuing play at the plate; cover dead-ball areas in case of an errant throw.

Batted ball to the outfield: You have the areas from F7 to the left-field dead-ball area and from F9 to the right-field dead-ball area. To right field: Trail B1 toward first base; rule fair/foul and catch/no catch as necessary. To left field: Move along the foul line or into the infield and rule fair/foul, catch/no catch as necessary; you are responsible for the lead runner if he tries to advance to third or home.

In order of importance, be prepared for the following situations:
1. A balk or illegal pitch.
2. The pitch: ball or strike.
3. Check-swings and defensive appeals.
4. A fair/foul call down either foul line.
5. A "trouble" ball in your area of the outfield.
6. All plays at home plate.
7. A double-play ball in the infield — observe and support U1.
8. A bunted ball when opponents converge — interference/obstruction.
9. An infield fly.

Case Study 23 — Pickoff throw to second

Game situation: Runners at first and second

Action on the field: Pitcher or catcher attempts pickoff at second base

RESPONSIBILITIES

Base umpire

(As F1 delivers, glance over your right shoulder to see if R2 is stealing.)

1. Read the pitcher's move to second base OR the catcher's throw after the pitch.

2. Step back with your left foot; keep your chest to the ball and let the throw turn you to second. If F1 releases a throw, use a cross-over step with your right foot and (if possible) move a step toward the cutout. (If F1 does not throw, he should remain in your field of vision.) If F2 makes the throw, you should have time for at least two cross-over steps before turning with the ball.

3. Read the throw; set; observe the play. *Timing!* Do not rule R2 out unless you are certain the fielder has complete control of the ball. If the play breaks down due to an overthrow, let the next throw take you to the next play, whether it is at second or third base.

4. If a rundown develops between second and third, you have full responsibility unless/until your partner communicates that he is in position to cover a play at third base; remember, there could be a throw or subsequent play on R1 advancing toward second.

5. If he is not retired, continue to observe R2 as long as the fielder has the ball.

Plate umpire

1. Read the pitcher's move to second base (observe the pitcher's entire pickoff move) OR call the pitch, then read the catcher's throw.

2. Clear the catcher and move a step or two toward third base.

3. Read the throw. If the throw is errant prepare to support your partner and to rule on an overthrow near a dead-ball area; if a rundown develops between second and third, move to the third-base cutout and communicate with your partner ("Bill, I've got this end!"). Remember you have responsibility for any play that develops at home plate.

Notes

MechaniGram™

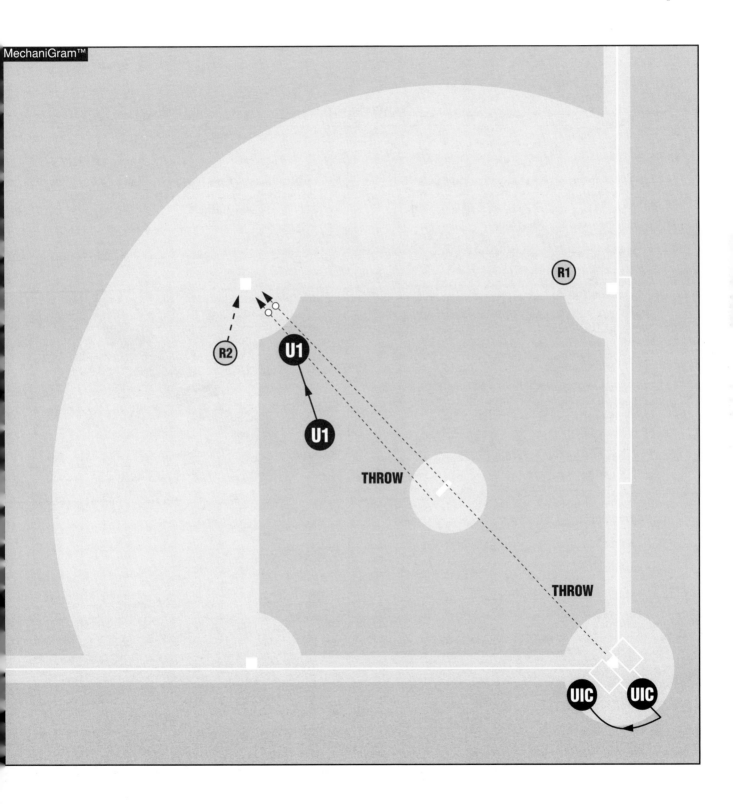

Case Study 24 — Pickoff throw to first

Game situation: Runners at first and second

Action on the field: Pitcher or catcher attempts pickoff at first base

RESPONSIBILITIES

Base umpire	Plate umpire
(As F1 delivers, glance over your right shoulder to see if R2 is stealing.) 1. Read the pitcher's move to first base OR the catcher's throw after the pitch. 2. Step directly toward the 45-foot line one to two steps. 3. Set. Observe the play. *Timing!* Do not rule R1 out unless you are certain F3 has complete control of the ball. 4. Be alert for a subsequent play: If R2 breaks for third base, you have primary responsibility; if F3 throws to second base it is your call; if the play breaks down due to a bad throw, prepare to lead R1 to second base but let the next throw take you to the play. 5. If he is not retired, continue to observe R1 as long as F3 has the ball.	1. Read the pitcher's move to first base (observe the pitcher's entire pickoff move) OR call the pitch, then read the catcher's throw. 3. Step back to obtain a clear view of the play at first base; observe the play. 4. Read the play. If the throw is errant, move toward the ball and rule on an overthrow near a dead-ball area; remember you have responsibility for any play that develops at home plate.

Notes

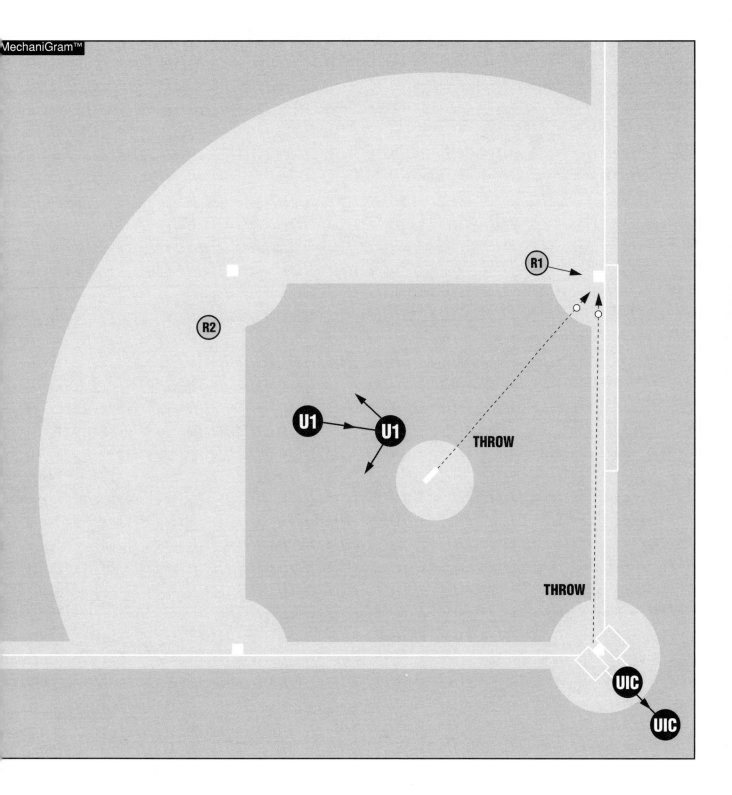

Case Study 25 — Third-base steal

Game situation: Runners at first and second

Action on the field: R2 is stealing

RESPONSIBILITIES

Base umpire	Plate umpire
(As F1 delivers, glance over your right shoulder to see if R2 is stealing.)	1. Call the pitch: ball or strike.

Base umpire

(As F1 delivers, glance over your right shoulder to see if R2 is stealing.)

1. Read the runner's break as you glance over your shoulder.

2. As soon as the pitch clears the batter, move aggressively toward the mid-point of the third-base line (half way between home and third). This will open the angle and give you a better view of the tag play at third. You want to establish a 90-degree angle between your line of sight and the runner's path to third base. BUT BEWARE: If R1 is also stealing, the catcher *could* throw to second and you would have to cover that play!

3. Let the throw turn you toward third base, set and observe the play.
NOTE: A third-base steal is among the most difficult plays for a two-man crew. Here's a hint: As you look to third, focus on the fielder's glove (instead of looking for the ball) and determine whether the glove tags the runner before the runner touches the base. If the tag is in time, wait to see the ball in the glove before you declare the runner out.

4. *Timing!* Do not rule R2 out unless you are certain the fielder has complete control of the ball.

5. Be alert for a subsequent play on R1, either at first base or at second base.

6. If he is not retired, continue to observe R2 as long as the fielder has the ball.

Plate umpire

1. Call the pitch: ball or strike.

2. Observe the action at home plate — is B1 guilty of interfering with F2's throw?

3. Read the throw. If the throw is errant, prepare to move toward the dead-ball area on the third-base side.

Notes

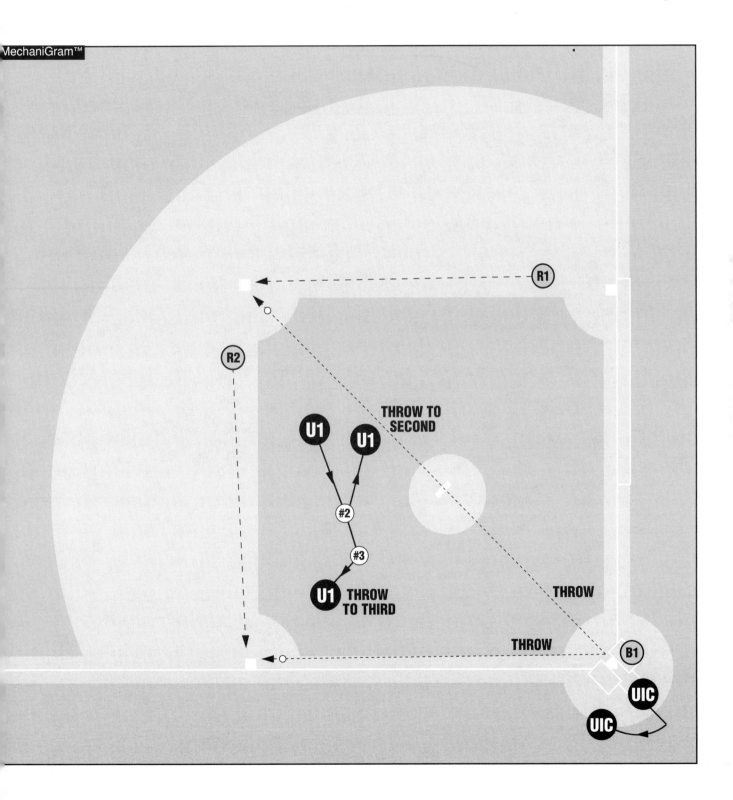

MechaniGram™

R1

R2

THROW TO
SECOND

U1   U1

#2

#3

U1   THROW
TO THIRD

THROW

THROW

B1

UIC

UIC

Case Study 26 — Routine fly ball in the "V"

Game situation: Runners at first and second

Action on the field: B1 flies to the middle of the outfield

RESPONSIBILITIES

Base umpire	Plate umpire
(As F1 delivers, glance over your right shoulder to see if R2 is stealing.)	1. Pause, read and react. Read the developing play and your partner.
1. Step up, turn and face the ball; pause, read and react. Read the position of the fielder making the play and determine whether this is a ball in your coverage area (it is) and whether this is a "trouble" ball (it is not).	2. With the ball in U1's coverage area, move half way up the third-base line in foul territory to observe the play. If R2 is tagging, move at least half-way to third base.
2. Since it is not a "trouble" ball: Move back two or three steps toward the pitcher's mound to "open" your field of view.	
3. If there is a catch (there is), signal only if the catch is made "below the knee"; verbally inform your partner of a routine catch. If a difficult play results in no catch, signal "safe" and verbally call, "No catch! No catch!"	4. After the catch: You have responsibility for any play that develops on R2 at third base and for any play that develops at home plate. If R2 commits to third, continue moving up the line and read the throw. If the throw is to third and a play develops, move into fair territory at the third-base cutout; establish your set position before the play occurs. *Timing!*
4. After the catch: You have tag-up responsibility at both first and second base. If R2 advances to third, the plate umpire has responsibility for the play; you have the play at second if R2 goes half way and returns. If R1 is "half way" to second, move toward the 45-foot line as you read the throw to the infield. If necessary, move into position for a developing play. If R1 is tagging to advance, move toward the second-base cutout as you read the throw. Establish your set position before the play occurs. *Timing!*	5. If R2 advances safely to third and the play ends, clear the runner before returning to home plate.
5. If a runner remains on base, observe the runner whenever the ball is near his location.	

Notes

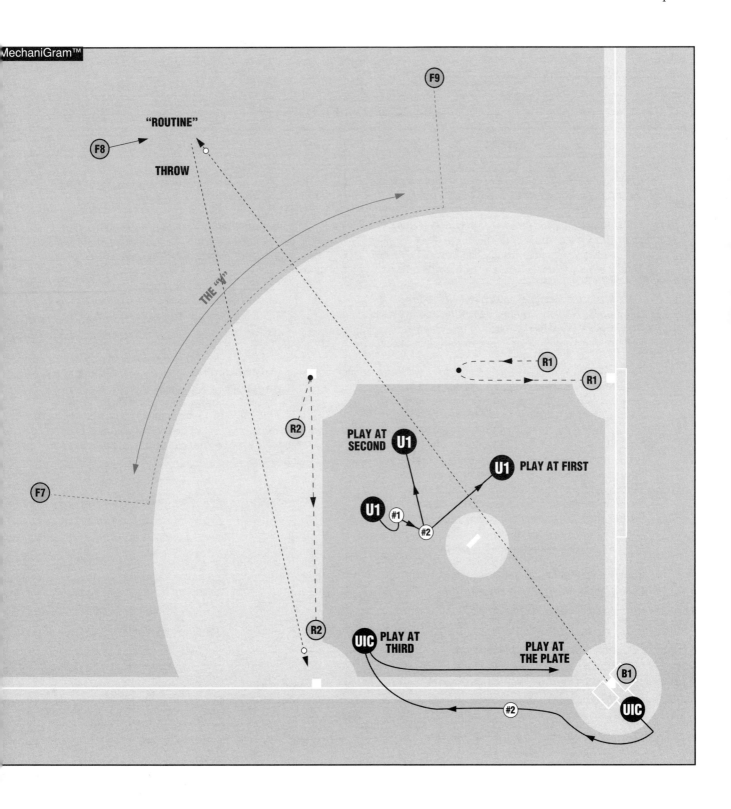

Case Study 27 — "Trouble" ball in the "V"

Game situation: Runners at first and second

Action on the field: B1 hits a "trouble" ball to the middle of the outfield

RESPONSIBILITIES

Base umpire	Plate umpire
(As F1 delivers, glance over your right shoulder to see if R2 is stealing.) 1. Step up, turn and face the ball; pause, read and react. Read the position of the fielder making the play and determine whether this is a ball in your coverage area (it is) and whether this is a "trouble" ball (it is). 2. Since it is a "trouble" ball: Move toward the coming play, but only to the edge of the infield grass. ***Do not leave the infield grass!*** *Timing!* When a difficult play does develop, after you are sure of the catch/no catch, "sell" your call. 3. If there is a catch, signal only if the catch is made "below the knee"; verbally inform your partner of a routine catch. If a difficult play results in no catch, signal "safe" and verbally call, "No catch! No catch!" 4. After the outfield play: Drop back several steps toward the mound, keeping your chest to the ball. You have all touches and tag-ups at both first and second base; you have all plays that develop at first, second and third (exception: A play on R2 at third). 5. As a subsequent play develops, if the play is your responsibility let the ball take you to the play. Establish your set position before the play occurs. *Timing!* Remember: Unless the inning ends, there could be another throw at any time. 6. If a runner remains on base, observe the runner whenever the ball is near his location.	1. Pause, read and react. Read the developing play and your partner. 2. With the ball in U1's coverage area, move half way up the third-base line in foul territory to observe the play. If R2 is tagging, move at least half-way to third base. 4. After the outfield play: You have responsibility for any play that develops on R2 at third base and for any play that develops at home plate. If R2 commits to third, continue moving up the line and read the throw. If the throw is to third and a play develops, move into fair territory at the third-base cutout; establish your set position before the play occurs. *Timing!* 6. If R2 advances safely to third and holds, when the play ends clear the runner before returning to home plate.

Notes

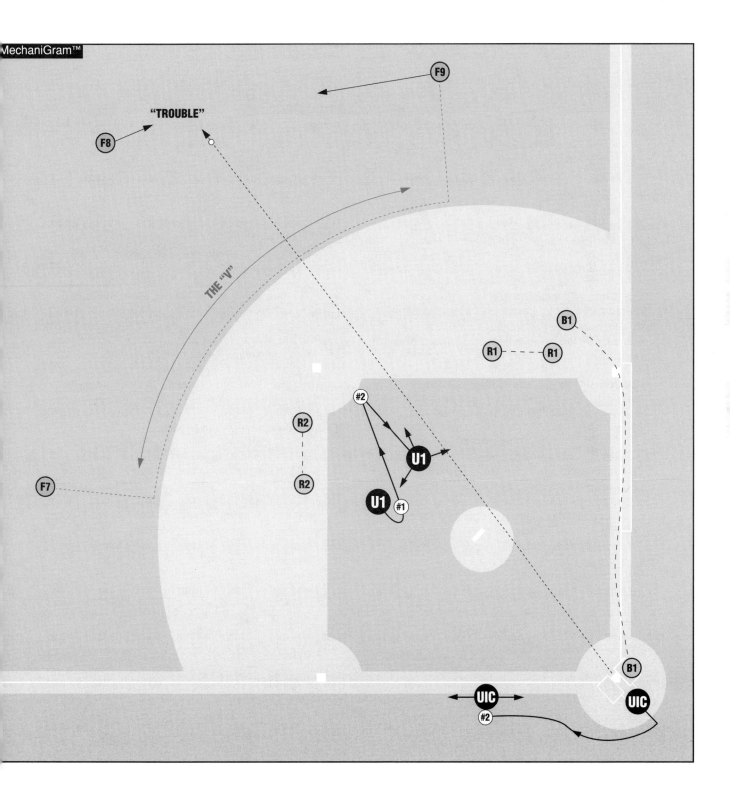

Case Study 28 — Infield fly

Game situation: Runners at first and second

Action on the field: B1 pops up

RESPONSIBILITIES

Base umpire

(As F1 delivers, glance over your right shoulder to see if R2 is stealing.)

1. Step up, turn and face the ball. Read the fielder who will make the play. (For a play involving a "trouble" ball, see Case Study 15, 16 or 17.)

3. Pause. Allow the ball to reach its maximum altitude, then determine whether it is an infield fly.

4. If the batted ball is behind the mound and clearly fair, you have *primary* responsibility for judging an infield fly. However either umpire may make the decision. If you are certain it is an infield fly, as the ball descends point straight up with your right hand and declare: "Infield fly, the batter is out!" (All force plays are now ended.)

5. Runners must tag up as on any *caught* batted ball. Whether caught or not, the ball remains alive: Prepare for subsequent plays on the bases.

6. When the play is over, observe runners whenever the ball is near their locations.

Plate umpire

1. Pause, read and react. Read the pop up and determine which fielder will make the play.

2. Clear the catcher. If fair/foul is a consideration, straddle the foul line; if fair/foul is not a consideration, move forward on the dirt in front of home plate and face the play.

3. Pause. Allow the ball to reach its maximum altitude, then determine whether it is an infield fly.

4. If the batted ball is in front of the mound or near a foul line, you have *primary* responsibility for judging an infield fly. However either umpire may make the decision. If you are certain it is an infield fly, as the ball descends point straight up with your right hand and declare: "Infield fly, the batter is out!" (All force plays are now ended.)

5. Runners must tag up as on any *caught* batted ball. Whether caught or not, the ball remains alive.

6. If a subsequent play develops, observe and be prepared to support your partner. In the event of an errant throw, you are responsible for watching R2 touch third and for any play that develops at home plate.

Communication: One umpire will be first to declare: "Infield fly, the batter is out." Immediately afterward, his partner will echo, "Infield Fly."

Notes

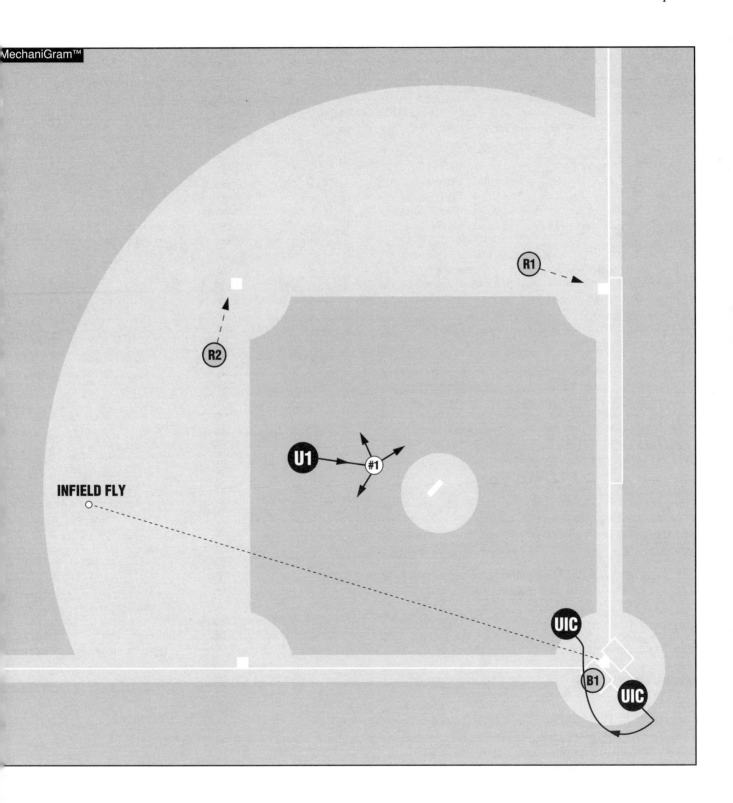

INFIELD FLY

Case Study 29 — Ground ball to the base umpire's right

Game situation: Runners at first and second

Action on the field: B1 hits ground ball played by F5 or F6

RESPONSIBILITIES

Base umpire

(As F1 delivers, glance over your right shoulder to see if R2 is stealing.)

1. Step up, turn and face the ball. Read ground ball and possible double play.

2. Realize there is always the possibility of a play at third base, either as the first play or as a subsequent play on a "surprise" throw to third by the pivot man. You are responsible for all plays at first, second and third base.

3. If the batted ball is fielded cleanly (it is), prepare for a double-play attempt.

4. As the infielder prepares to make the first throw, keep your chest to the ball as you move two or three steps toward Position B (you will be moving backward). Let the infielder's throw to second base turn your shoulders square to the bag. Stop and set before the ball arrives at second. *Determine* safe/out of R1. (*Timing!* Do not rule R1 out unless the fielder has complete control of the ball.)

5. Turn slightly (chest to right field or the right field corner); observe the remaining action at second base as you move toward the first base line (as far as the play will allow, usually two or three steps) and prepare for the relay to first. *Declare* R1 out or safe, aloud, *while moving* toward the first base line.

6. Let the relay throw turn you toward first base. (The play at first will happen very quickly, so be prepared.)

7. Set for the play at first and observe the play. *Timing!* Do not rule B1 out unless the fielder has complete control of the ball.

8. When the play is over, if a runner remains on base, observe the runner whenever the ball is near his location.

NOTE: Proper timing on the turn to first will keep your eyes on the ball until the fielder makes the relay throw. If the play breaks down (dropped ball, errant throw, interference at second) move directly to second base and "sell" your out or safe decision with an emphatic voice-and-signal combination.

Plate umpire

1. Pause, read and react. Read the possible double-play ball.

2. Clear the catcher; if the ball is hit near the third-base line, straddle the line and observe the play. You must first rule fair or foul.

3. If fair/foul is not a concern, move a few feet toward third, but *stay home*.

4. You are responsible for watching R2 touch third, and for any play that develops at home plate.

7. If a subsequent play develops at first base, observe. Rule immediately on interference by B1 or an overthrow; offer your opinion of a swipe tag or pulled foot only if U1 requests help.

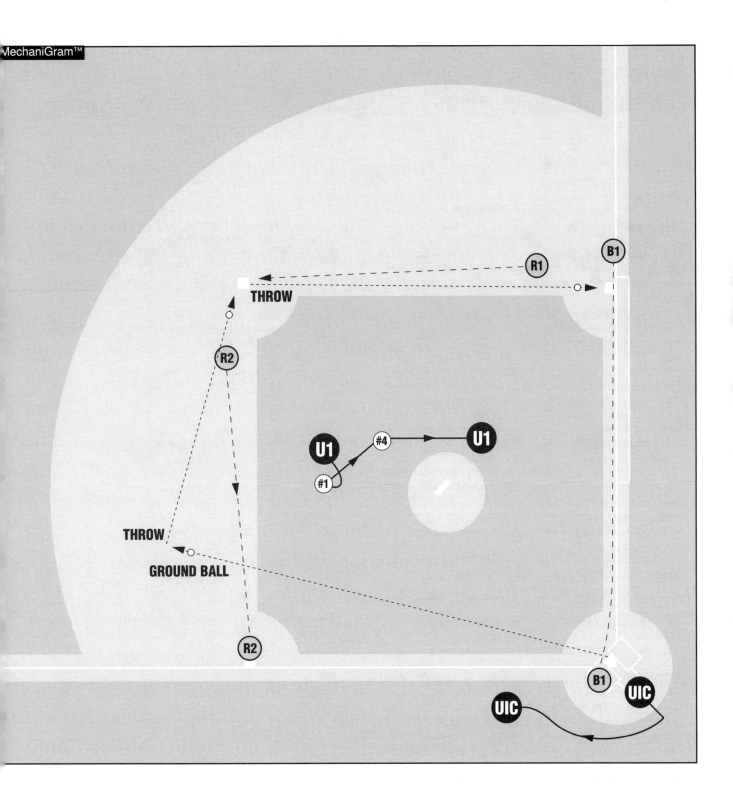

Case Study 30 — Ground ball to the base umpire's left

Game situation: Runners at first and second

Action on the field: B1 hits ground ball played by F1, F3 or F4

RESPONSIBILITIES

Base umpire	Plate umpire
(As F1 delivers, glance over your right shoulder to see if R2 is stealing.) 1. Step up, turn and face the ball. Read ground ball and possible double play.	1. Pause, read and react. Read the possible double-play ball.
2. Realize the possibility of a play at third base exists, but is diminished if F3 or F4 field the batted ball. You are responsible for all plays at first, second and third base.	2. Clear the catcher; if the ball is hit near the first-base line, straddle the line and observe the play. You must first rule fair or foul.
3. If the batted ball is fielded cleanly (it is), prepare for a double-play attempt.	3. If fair/foul is not a concern, move a few feet toward third base, but *stay home*.
4. As the infielder prepares to make the first throw, keep your chest to the ball as you move several steps toward Position B (you will be moving forward). Let the infielder's throw to second base turn your shoulders square to the bag. Stop and set before the ball arrives at second. *Determine* safe/out of R1. (*Timing!* Do not rule R1 out unless the fielder has complete control of the ball.)	4. You are responsible for watching R2 touch third, and for any play that develops at home plate.
5. Turn slightly (chest to right field or the right field corner); observe the remaining action at second base as you move toward the first base line (as far as the play will allow, usually two or three steps) and prepare for the relay to first. *Declare* R1 out or safe, aloud, *while moving* toward the first base line.	
6. Let the relay throw turn you toward first base. (The play at first will happen very quickly, so be prepared.)	
7. Set for the play at first and observe the play. *Timing!* Do not rule B1 out unless the fielder has complete control of the ball.	7. If a subsequent play develops at first base, observe. Rule immediately on interference by B1 or an overthrow; offer your opinion of a swipe tag or pulled foot only if U1 requests help.
8. When the play is over, if a runner remains on base, observe the runner whenever the ball is near his location.	
NOTE: Proper timing on the turn to first will keep your eyes on the ball until the fielder makes the relay throw. If the play breaks down (dropped ball, errant throw, interference at second) move directly to second base and "sell" your out or safe decision with an emphatic voice-and-signal combination.	

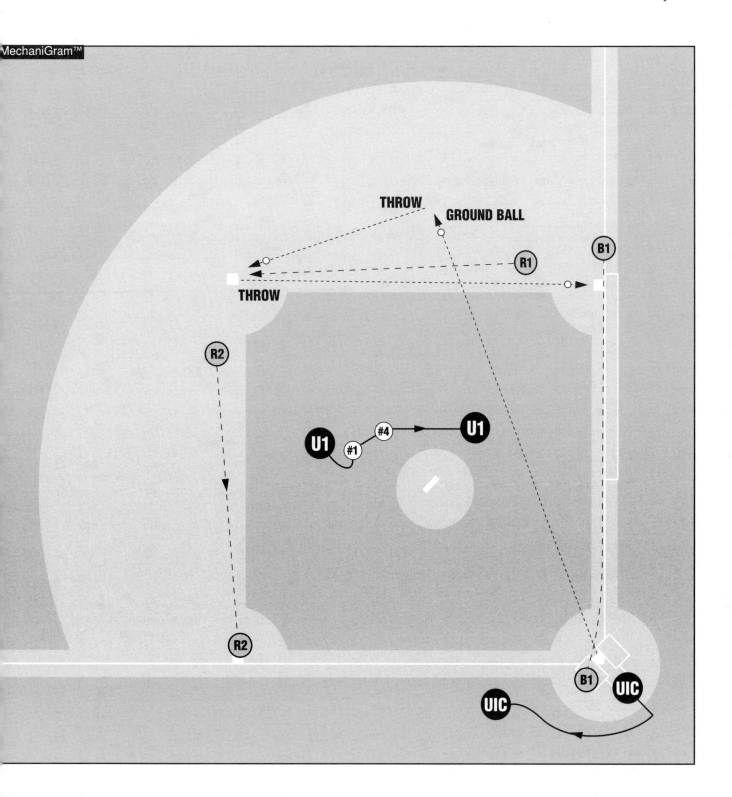

Case Study 31 — Ground ball in the hole between short and third

Game situation: Runners at first and second

Action on the field: B1 hits ground ball played by F6

RESPONSIBILITIES

Base umpire	Plate umpire
(As F1 delivers, glance over your right shoulder to see if R2 is stealing.)	1. Pause, read and react. Read the possible double-play ball.
1. Step up, turn and face the ball. Read ground ball and possible double play.	2. Clear the catcher. Move a few feet toward third, but *stay home*.
2. Realize there is always the possibility of a play at third base, either as the first play or as a subsequent play on a throw to third by the pivot man. You are responsible for all plays at first, second and third base.	
3. If the batted ball is fielded by F6 moving toward the left-field line (it is), be particularly alert for a throw to third.	4. When the first play develops at third, it is the base umpire's responsibility. Observe, particularly for a pulled foot by an inexperienced third baseman. Offer your opinion only if U1 requests help.
4. When F6 prepares to throw to third, keep your chest to the ball and move aggressively toward the midpoint of the line between home and third.	5. In the event of an errant throw, you are responsible for watching R2 touch third and for any play that develops at home plate.
5. Read the throw. Stop and set before the ball arrives at third. *Timing!* Do not rule R2 out unless the fielder has complete control of the ball.	
6. Remain alert. When the first play is at third, subsequent plays are rare, but they do occur.	7. If a subsequent play develops, observe and be prepared to support your partner.
7. When the play is over, observe runners whenever the ball is near their locations.	

Notes

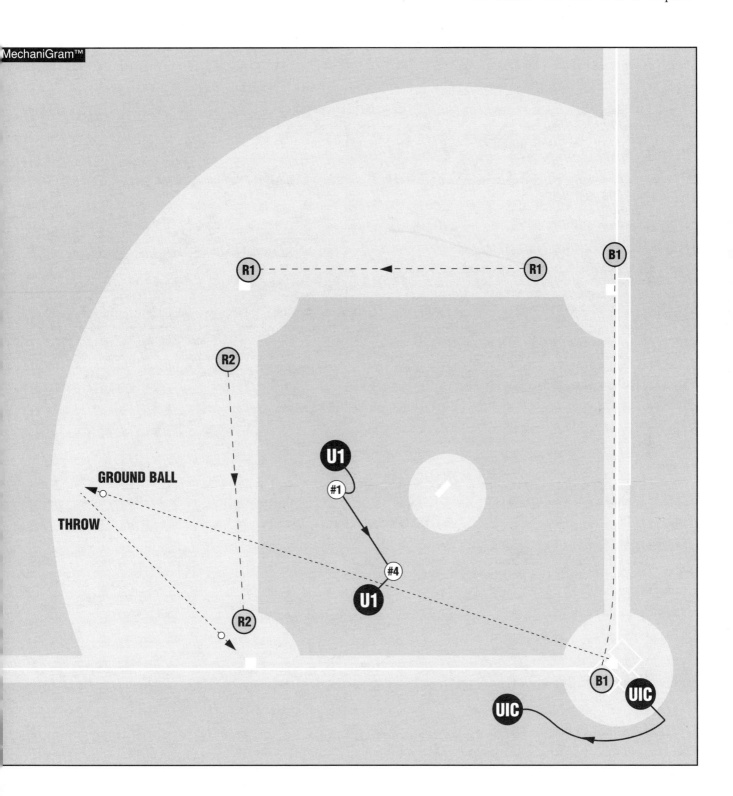

Case Study 32 — Base hit to the outfield

Game situation: Runners at first and second

Action on the field: Clean hit to the outfield

RESPONSIBILITIES

Base umpire	Plate umpire
(As F1 delivers, glance over your right shoulder to see if R2 is stealing.) 1. Step up, turn and face the ball; pause, read and react. Read "hit." 2. Move back two or three steps toward the pitcher's mound to "open" your field of view. 4. Remain aware of the status of the ball as you observe both R1 and B1 advancing to touch bases; observe R2's touch at third base only if UIC is "on the line" to determine fair/foul to right field. 6. As the ball returns to the infield, you are responsible for any play that develops at first, second or third. Let the throw take you to the play, move aggressively into position, and set before the play occurs. 7. When runners remain on base, observe carefully whenever the ball is near a runner's location.	1. Pause, read and react. Read "hit." 2. Clear the catcher. 3. If fair/foul is a consideration on a ball hit to right field, communicate with your partner: "I'm on the line!" Move aggressively along the first-base line, set before the play occurs and rule fair or foul. 4. In all other cases, remain in foul territory as you move a few feet up the third-base line, but *stay home*. 5. Observe R2 touching third base; prepare for any play that develops at home plate.

Notes

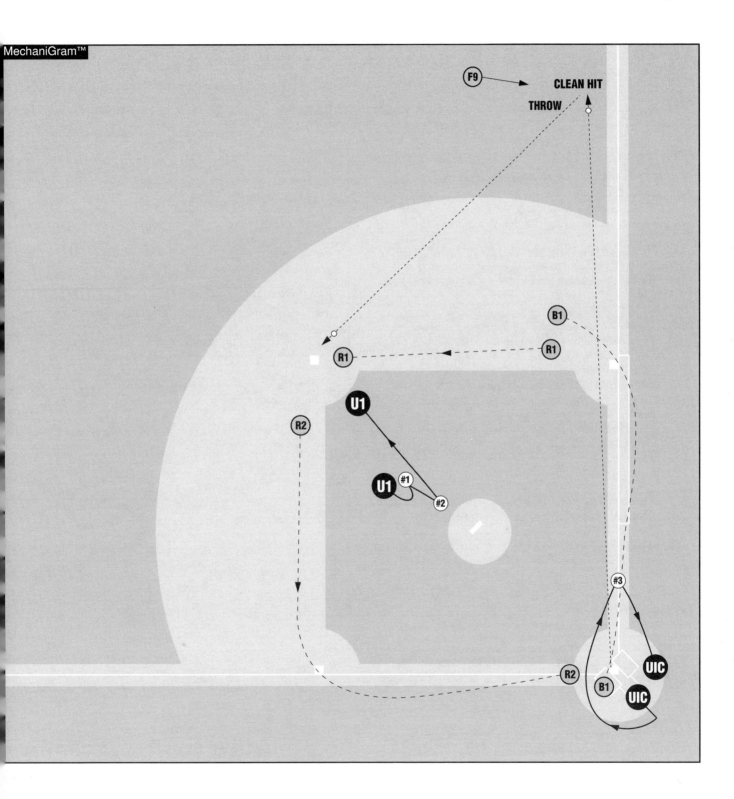

Case Study 33 — Bunt

Game situation: Runners at first and second

Action on the field: B1 bunts

RESPONSIBILITIES

Base umpire	Plate umpire
(As F1 delivers, glance over your right shoulder to see if R2 is stealing.)	1. Pause, read and react. Read the bunted ball, usually in "the box."
1. Step up, turn and face the ball; pause, read and react. Read the bunted ball, usually in "the box."	2. Clear the catcher; rule fair or foul as necessary.
2. Read whether the play will develop at first, second or third base; react by moving aggressively two or three steps toward the play. In any event, you have the first play.	
	4. Move out to the catcher's left; read the throw and whether the play is at first, second or third base.
3. Move to establish a 90-degree angle to the expected throw, but avoid stepping into the path of *any* throw.	5. On a play at first base, observe the action and rule immediately if there is interference by B1.
4. Read the throw. On a good throw, come to your set position and focus on the play; on a bad throw, adjust to a position which will afford the best possible view of the play. For a play at first base, you'll move across the infield behind the mound, then try to move closer to the 45-foot line (if time permits); for a play at second base, move near the cutout; for a play at third, move toward the mid-point of the third-base line.	6. Offer your opinion of a swipe tag or pulled foot at first base only if U1 requests help.
	7. Realize you have responsibility for any play at home plate.
5. *Timing!* Do not rule the runner out unless you are certain the fielder has complete control of the ball. If the play breaks down and you are uncertain of a tag or pulled foot, decide whether your partner may be able to assist; communicate with UIC *before* you rule B1 safe or out.	
7. No matter where the first play develops, recognize the possibility of a subsequent play. You have responsibility for any play at first, second or third base.	

Notes

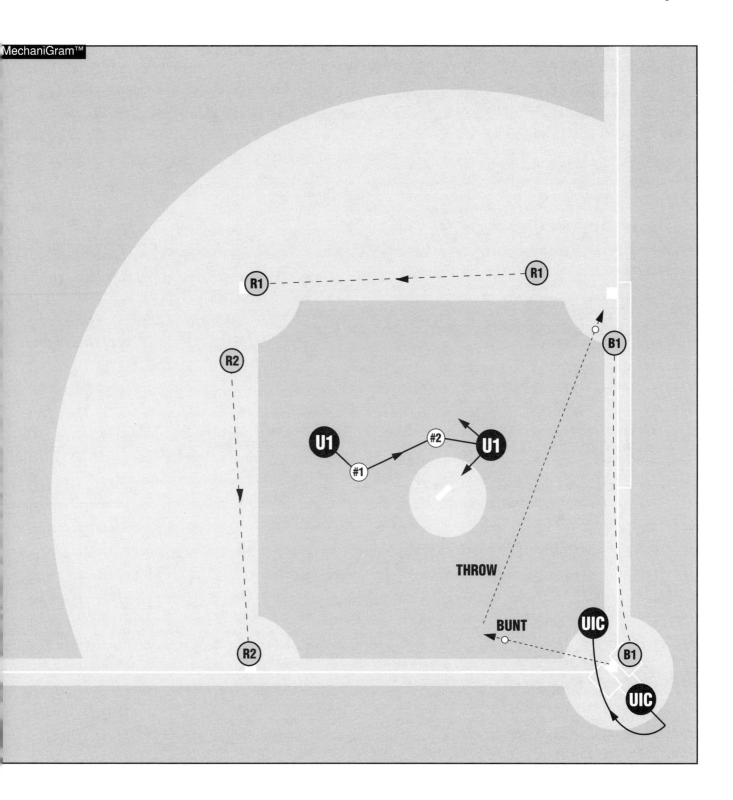

Review: Runners at first and second

Base umpire
• Start in position C.
• Adjust based on the game situation (bunt, steal, etc.), defensive tendencies and the lead runner's baserunning ability.
• Fair/foul: You have no responsibility.
• Field coverage: You have the "V," beginning with any ball hit directly to F7 and ending with any ball hit directly to F9.
• On the bases: You have all plays at first, second and third base *except*: UIC will cover R2 advancing to third after tagging up on a fly ball (unless UIC is on the first-base line to determine fair/foul or catch/no catch).
• Priorities:
    1. A balk or illegal pitch.
    2. Pick off attempt at second base by the pitcher.
    3. Pick off attempt at first base by the pitcher.
    4. Help for the plate umpire on the half-swing.
    5. A third-base steal — as F1 delivers, glance over your right shoulder to see if R2 is breaking for third.
    6. A double-steal and an unexpected first play at second base.
    7. Pick off attempt at first base by the catcher.
    8. Pickoff attempt at second base by the catcher.
    9. A "trouble ball" in your area of the outfield — the "V," beginning with any ball hit directly to F7 and ending with any ball hit directly to F9.
    10. A ground ball in the infield: You have all plays at first, second and third; UIC will "stay home" to observe R2 touching third and will cover all plays at the plate.
    11. A batted or bunted ball with F1, F3, F4 and/or B1 converging at the base.
    12. A ball hit to the outfield followed by a play on B1 or R1 at any base.
    13. An infield fly.

Umpire in chief
• Your first concern is always the pitch: strike or ball.
• Fair/foul: You have all fair/foul decisions.
• Field coverage: You have balls hit to the outfield to the left or right of the "V."
• On the bases: You have all plays at home plate; you also have a play on R2 tagging up and advancing to third (unless a fair/foul or catch/no catch decision requires you to be on the first-base line).
• Priorities:
    1. A balk or illegal pitch.
    2. The pitch: ball or strike.
    3. Check-swings and defensive appeals.
    4. A fair/foul call down either foul line.
    5. A "trouble" ball in your area of the outfield.
    6. All plays at home plate.
    7. A double-play ball in the infield — observe and support U1.
    8. A bunted ball when opponents converge — interference/obstruction.
    9. An infield fly.

Quiz
Without referring back, you should be able to answer the following true-false questions. Remember: R1 is always the runner who begins a play at first base; R2 at second; R3 at third; B1 is the batter-runner; fielders are identified by their scoring abbreviations (F1 is the pitcher, F2 the catcher, etc.).

1. When an infield fly occurs, only one umpire should declare the infield fly.
2. On a third-base steal, U1 will move directly toward the mid-point of the third-base line.
3. If U1 commits to third to cover a steal, UIC *may* rule on a surprise throw to second base.
4. Any time R2 tags up and advances on a caught fly ball, UIC makes the call on the play at third base.
5. On a double play ball, U1 will decide whether R1 is safe or out while moving toward first base.
6. Either umpire may call a balk or an illegal pitch.

Runner configuration: Bases loaded

Base umpire position: Position C.

   Adjustment factors: With the bases loaded, the offense has few options. That limits your adjustments, but allows you to take a "deep" position for a wider field of view at the time of the pitch.

   Defensive position: If the infielders are playing "in," you'll find yourself between F6 and the second-base cutout; insure your position will not hinder his opportunity to field a batted ball.

   Catcher tendencies: Some "gambling" teams will allow the catcher to attempt pickoff throws with the bases loaded. If that fits the defense, you'll at least be alert for a catcher's pickoff.

In order of importance, be prepared for the following situations:
   1. A balk or illegal pitch by the pitcher.
   2. Help for the plate umpire on the check-swing.
   3. A pickoff attempt by the pitcher or catcher.
   4. A "trouble ball" in your area of the outfield.
   5. A ground ball play — multiple possibilities.
   6. A batted or bunted ball with F3, F1 and B1 all converging at the base.
   7. A clean hit, or any batted ball to your area of the outfield.
   8. An infield fly.

Plate umpire anticipation:
Your initial position is always behind the plate. As the pitcher begins his delivery, come set in your stance. Your initial responsibility is always calling the pitch a strike or a ball. Respond to the batted ball and the action as it develops.

   Batted ball in the infield: Stay home. Straddle the foul line or the foul line extended as necessary to determine fair/foul; prepare for a force play at the plate; cover dead-ball areas in case of an errant throw. Be aware of the defensive alignment: If the infield is "in" or "corners up," the first play is likely to be at the plate; if the infield is "back" or at "double-play depth," a first play at the plate is unlikely.

   Batted ball to the outfield: *Stay home.* If fair/foul or catch/no catch are a consideration, move a few steps toward the developing play, but realize you must return to home for a play at the plate. Otherwise, move toward the third-base dugout, observe R3 tagging up and/or R2 touching third, and prepare for a play at the plate.

In order of importance, be prepared for the following situations:
   1. A balk or illegal pitch.
   2. The pitch: ball or strike.
   3. Check-swings and defensive appeals.
   4. A fair/foul call down either foul line.
   5. A "trouble" ball in your umpire's area of the outfield: cover the batted ball and return to the plate for a developing play.
   6. A bunted ball when opponents converge — interference/obstruction.
   7. An infield fly.

Case Study 34 — Routine fly ball in the "V"

Game situation: Bases loaded

Action on the field: B1 flies to the middle of the outfield

RESPONSIBILITIES

Base umpire	Plate umpire
1. Step up, turn and face the ball; pause, read and react. Read the position of the fielder making the play and determine whether this is a ball in your coverage area (it is) and whether this is a "trouble" ball (it is not).	1. Pause, read and react. Read the developing play and your partner.
2. Since it is not a "trouble" ball: Move back two or three steps toward the pitcher's mound to "open" your field of view. Insure that your position does not hinder the fielder's potential throw to any base.	2. With the ball in U1's coverage area, move toward the third-base dugout and open your field of view. You must observe the catch and R3's tag-up at third base.
3. If there is a catch (there is), signal only if the catch is made "below the knee"; verbally inform your partner of a routine catch. If a difficult play results in no catch, signal "safe" and verbally call, "No catch! No catch!"	4. After the outfield play: You have responsibility for any play that develops at home plate. *Timing!*
4. After the catch: You have tag-up responsibility at both first and second base *and* any play that develops at first, second or third base. Keep your chest to the ball and let the throw take you to the next play. Establish your set position before the play occurs. *Timing!*	
5. As a subsequent play develops, if the play is your responsibility let the ball take you to the play. Establish your set position before the play occurs. *Timing!* Remember: Unless the inning ends, there could be another throw at any time.	
6. If a runner remains on base, observe the runner whenever the ball is near his location.	

Notes

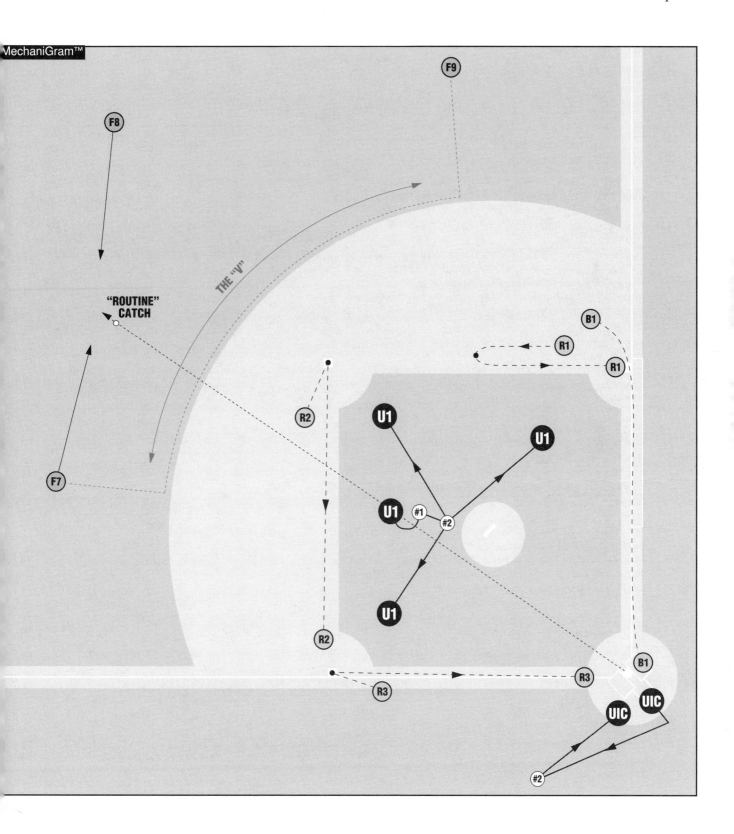

Case Study 35 — "Trouble" ball in the "V"

Game situation: Bases loaded

Action on the field: B1 hits a "trouble" ball to the middle of the outfield

RESPONSIBILITIES

Base umpire

1. Step up, turn and face the ball; pause, read and react. Read the position of the fielder making the play and determine whether this is a ball in your coverage area (it is) and whether this is a "trouble" ball (it is).

2. Since it is a "trouble" ball: Move toward the developing play, but only to the edge of the infield grass. **Do not leave the infield grass!** *Timing!* When a difficult play does develop, after you are sure of the catch/no catch, "sell" your call.

3. If there is a catch, signal only if the catch is made "below the knee"; verbally inform your partner of a routine catch. If a difficult play results in no catch, signal "safe" and verbally call, "No catch! No catch!"

4. After the outfield play: Drop back several steps toward the mound, keeping your chest to the ball and insuring that your position never hinders a fielder's potential throw to any base. You have all touches and tag-ups at both first and second base; you have all plays that develop at first, second and third.

5. As a subsequent play develops, if the play is your responsibility let the ball take you to the play. Establish your set position before the play occurs. *Timing!* Remember: Unless the inning ends, there could be another throw at any time.

6. If a runner remains on base, observe the runner whenever the ball is near his location.

Plate umpire

1. Pause, read and react. Read the developing play and your partner.

2. With the ball in U1's coverage area, move toward the third-base dugout and open your field of view. You must observe the catch and R3's tag-up at third base.

4. After the outfield play: You have responsibility for any play that develops at home plate. *Timing!*

Notes

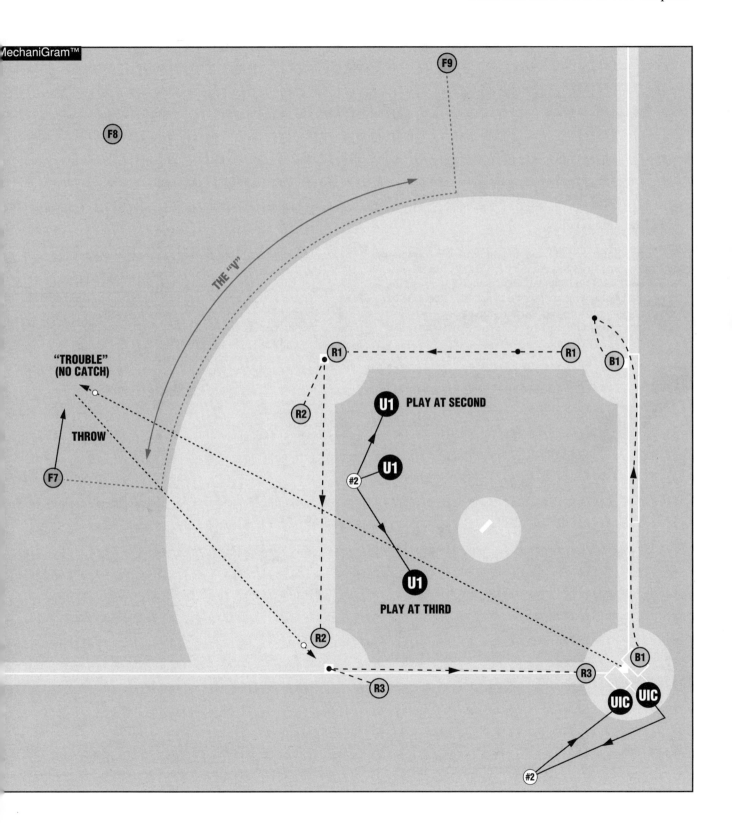

Case Study 36 — Fly ball to left field

Game situation: Bases loaded

Action on the field: Left fielder moves toward the line on a fly ball

RESPONSIBILITIES

Base umpire	Plate umpire
1. Step up, turn and face the ball; pause, read and react. Read the position of the fielder making the play and determine whether this is a ball in your coverage area (it is not).	1. Pause, read and react. Read the position of the fielder making the play and determine whether this is a ball in your coverage area (it is) and whether this is a "trouble" ball.
2. Since the ball is not in your area: Move back two or three steps toward the back of the pitcher's mound to "open" your field of view. Remain aware of the fly ball status as you observe R1 and R2 (who may be tagging up), and B1 touching first base. Listen for your partner to inform you of a catch.	2. Since the ball is in your coverage area, clear the catcher and communicate with your partner: "I've got the ball!" If fair/foul is a consideration or if it is a "trouble" ball, you'll have to establish a position near the third-base line with an unobstructed view of the fielder making the play, but *stay near home!* If fair/foul is not a consideration and it is not a "trouble" ball, move toward the third-base dugout to observe the play. This will open your angle and let you observe the fielder's catch and R3 tagging up. You are responsible for any play that develops at home plate.
	3. Develop the best angle possible to observe the catch/no catch.
5. After the play in the outfield: You are responsible for any play at first, second and third base; UIC observes R3 tagging up and then stays home. Establish your set position before the play occurs. *Timing!*	4. If there is a catch (there is), signal only if the catch is made "below the knee"; verbally inform your partner of any catch: "Bill, that's a catch."
6. If a runner remains on base, observe the runner whenever the ball is near his location.	5. After the outfield play: You have responsibility for any play that develops at home plate. If R3 tries to score, return to home plate and read the throw. If a play develops at the plate, establish your set position before the play occurs. *Timing!*

Notes

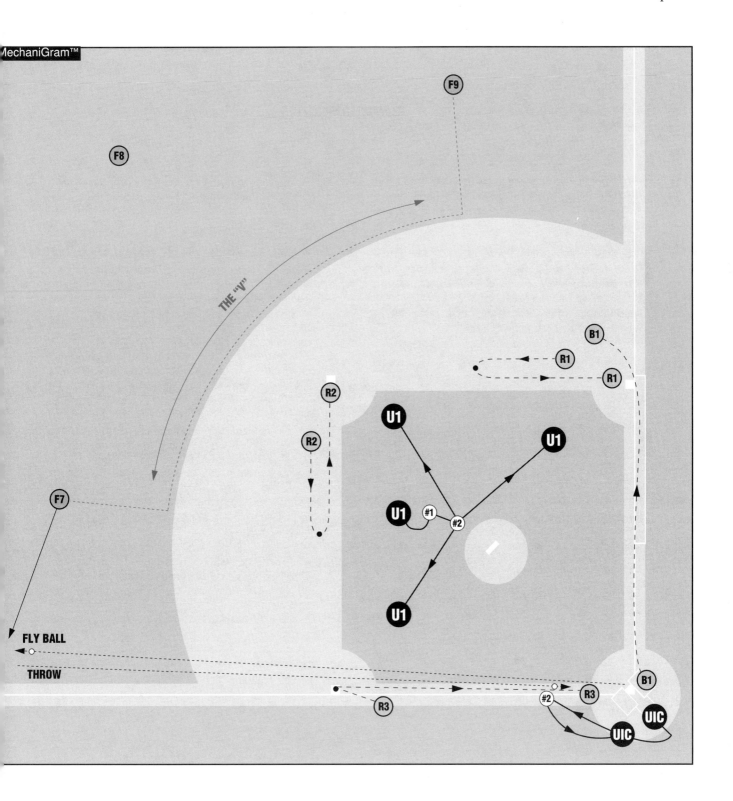

Case Study 37 — Fly ball to right field

Game situation: Bases loaded

Action on the field: Right fielder moves toward the line on a fly ball

RESPONSIBILITIES

Base umpire	Plate umpire
1. Step up, turn and face the ball; pause, read and react. Read the position of the fielder making the play and determine whether this is a ball in your coverage area (it is not).	1. Pause, read and react. Read the position of the fielder making the play and determine whether this is a ball in your coverage area (it is) and whether this is a "trouble" ball.
2. Since the ball is not in your area: Move back two or three steps toward the back of the pitcher's mound to "open" your field of view. Remain aware of the fly ball status as you observe R1 and R2 (who may be tagging up), and B1 touching first base. Listen for your partner to inform you of a catch.	2. Since the ball is in your coverage area, clear the catcher and communicate with your partner: "I've got the ball!" If fair/foul is a consideration or if it is a "trouble" ball, move a short distance up the first-base line to observe the play. You must remain close enough to home plate to return in time to be in position for a play at the plate if R3 tags up or tries to score. Your first priority is the batted ball; after you determine fair/foul and catch/no catch, take a quick glance toward the runner tagging up at third base. It is a difficult look. Remember: Your first priority is the ball! If fair/foul is not a consideration and it is not a "trouble" ball, move toward the third-base dugout to observe the play. This will open your angle and let you observe the fielder's catch and R3 tagging up. You are responsible for any play that develops at home plate.
5. After the play in the outfield: You are responsible for any play at first, second and third base; UIC observes R3 tagging up and then stays home. Establish your set position before the play occurs. *Timing!*	3. Develop the best angle possible to observe the catch/no catch.
6. If a runner remains on base, observe the runner whenever the ball is near his location.	4. If there is a catch (there is), signal only if the catch is made "below the knee"; verbally inform your partner of any catch: "Bill, that's a catch."
	5. After the outfield play: You have responsibility for any play that develops at home plate. If R3 tries to score, return to home plate and read the throw. If a play develops at the plate, establish your set position before the play occurs. *Timing!*

Notes

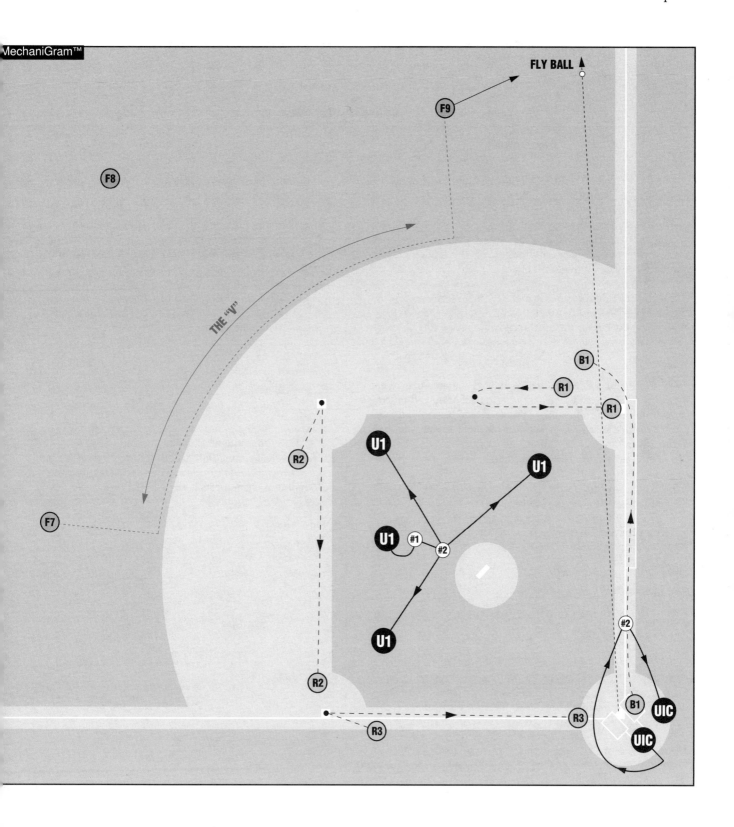

Case Study 38 — Ground ball in the infield

Game situation: bases loaded
Action on the field: B1 hits ground ball played by an infielder

RESPONSIBILITIES

Base umpire

1. Step up, turn and face the ball. Read ground ball and possible double play. You have responsibility for all plays that develop at first, second and third base.

2. If the batted ball is fielded cleanly (it is), prepare for a double-play attempt, but be certain your position on the infield never hinders a potential throw to the plate.

3. As the infielder prepares to make the first throw, keep your chest to the ball as you move cautiously toward the back of the mound. Let the infielder's throw turn you square to the base. Stop and set before the ball arrives; *determine* safe or out. (*Timing!* Do not rule R1 out unless the fielder has complete control of the ball.)

4. If the first play develops at second base, a double-play attempt is very likely: Turn slightly (chest to right field or the right field corner); observe the remaining action at second base as you move toward the first base line (as far as the play will allow, usually two or three steps) and prepare for the relay to first. *Declare* R1 out or safe, aloud, *while moving* toward the first base line.

5. Let the relay throw turn you toward first base. (The play at first will happen very quickly, so be prepared.)

6. Come to hands-on-knees set for play at first and observe the play.

7. *Timing!* Do not rule B1 out unless the fielder has complete control of the ball.

8. When the play is over, observe each the runner whenever the ball is near his location.

NOTE: If the first infield play is at home plate, read the catcher. As necessary, move aggressively toward the 45-foot line and prepare for a subsequent play at first base. If the first play is at third base or first base, rule on that play and read the covering fielder. Prepare for a subsequent play at second (the next "short" throw in your area of responsibility) or at the opposite corner of the diamond.
NOTE: On a "normal" double play, proper timing on the turn to first will keep your eyes on the ball until the fielder makes the relay throw. If the play breaks down (dropped ball, errant throw, interference at second) move directly to second base and "sell" your out or safe decision with an emphatic voice-and-signal combination.

Plate umpire

1. Pause, read and react. Read the possible double-play ball.

2. Clear the catcher; if the ball is hit near either foul line: Move into foul territory, take a position straddling the foul line extended and observe the play. You must first rule fair or foul.

3. If fair/foul is not a concern, move a few feet toward third base, but *stay home*. You are responsible for any play that develops at home plate.

6. If the subsequent play develops at first base, observe. Rule immediately on interference by B1 or an overthrow; offer your opinion of a swipe tag or pulled foot only if U1 requests help.

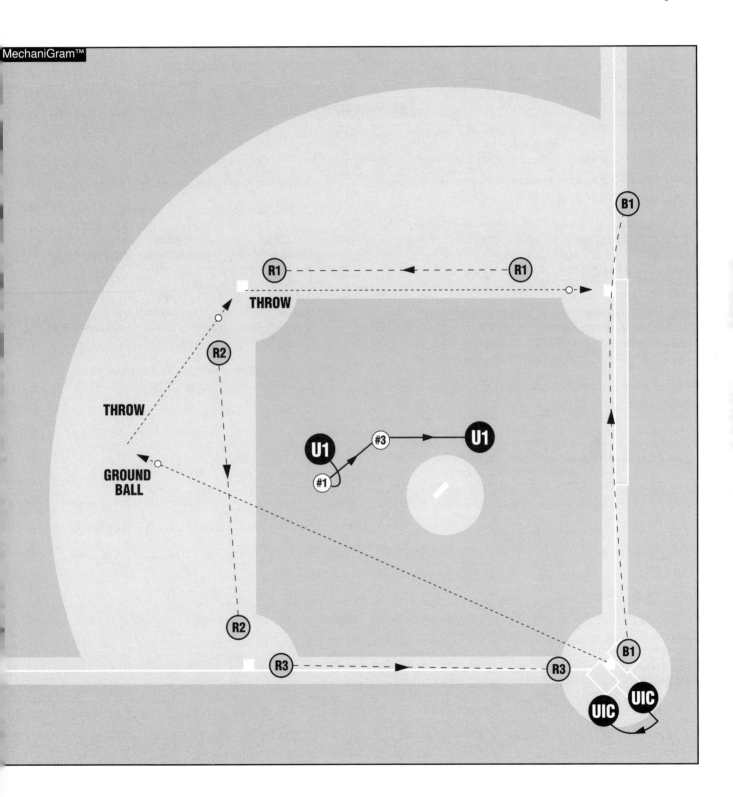

Case Study 39 — Base hit to the outfield

Game situation: Bases loaded

Action on the field: Clean hit to the outfield

RESPONSIBILITIES

Base umpire	Plate umpire
1. Step up, turn and face the ball; pause, read and react. Read "hit."	1. Pause, read and react. Read "hit."
2. Move back two or three steps toward the pitcher's mound to "open" your field of view.	2. Clear the catcher.
	3. If fair/foul is a consideration, assume a position on the foul line extended, set before the play occurs and rule fair or foul; you also must observe R3 touching home plate.
4. Remain aware of the status of the ball as you observe both R1 and B1 advancing to touch bases; observe R2's touch at third base only if UIC is "on the line" to determine fair/foul to right field.	4. In all other cases, remain in foul territory as you move a few feet up the third-base line and observe R3 touching home plate, but *stay home*.
	5. Observe R2 touching third and prepare for any play that develops at home plate.
6. As the ball returns to the infield, you are responsible for any play that develops at first, second or third. Let the throw lead you to the play, move aggressively into position, and set before the play occurs. *Timing!*	
7. When runners remain on base, observe carefully whenever the ball is near a runner's location.	

Notes

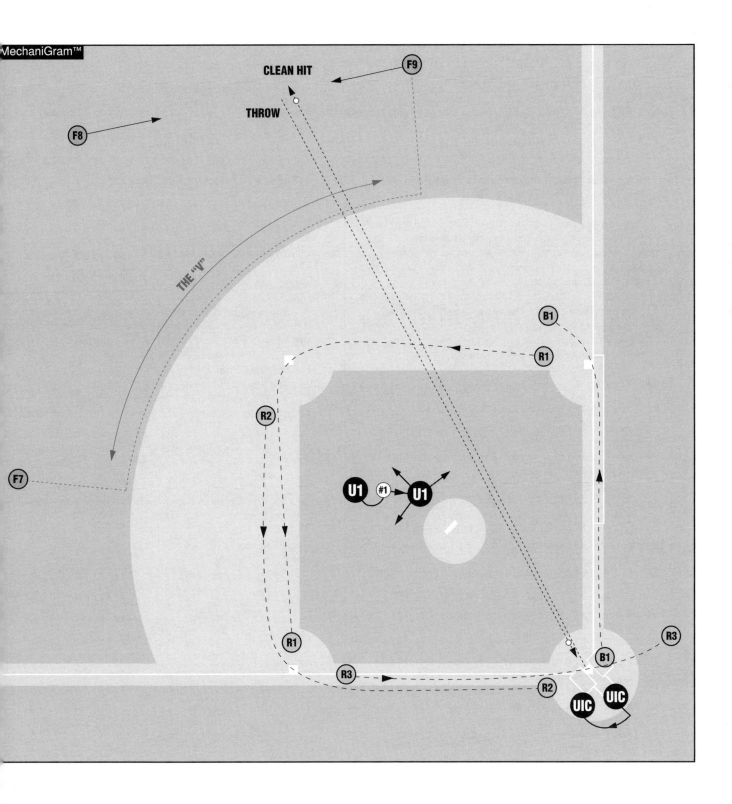

Case Study 40 — Bunt

Game situation: Bases loaded

Action on the field: B1 bunts

RESPONSIBILITIES

Base umpire

1. Step up, turn and face the ball; pause, read and react. Read the bunted ball, usually in "the box."

2. Read the fielders and determine where the play will develop (normally at either home plate or first base). If the play develops at first, second or third, move aggressively two or three steps toward the play. You have all plays at first, second and third base.

3. Move to establish a 90-degree angle to the expected throw, but avoid stepping into the path of *any* throw.

4. Read the throw; let the throw turn you to the developing play. On a good throw, come to your set position and focus on the play; on a bad throw, adjust to a position which will afford the best possible view of the play. For a play at first base, you'll move across the infield behind the mound, then try to move closer to the 45-foot line (if time permits); for a play at second base, move near the cutout; for a play at third, move toward the mid-point of the third-base line.

5. *Timing!* In all cases, do not rule the runner out unless you are certain the fielder has complete control of the ball. If the play breaks down and you are uncertain of a tag or pulled foot, decide whether your partner may be able to assist. If the play is at first base, communicate with UIC *before* you rule B1 safe or out.

7. No matter where the first play develops, recognize the possibility of a subsequent play. If the first play is at home, a subsequent play is likely at first base. Adjust by making a preliminary move behind the mound (as the play at the plate develops), then read the throw to first base. If that play develops, move aggressively toward the 45-foot line and set.

Plate umpire

1. Pause, read and react. Read the bunted ball, usually in "the box."

2. Clear the catcher; rule fair or foul as necessary.

3. Move out to the catcher's left. Read the fielders and determine where the first play will develop. Prepare for a force play at the plate.

4. If the first play develops at home plate, observe the developing play and set before the play. *Timing!* Remember, it is a force play; it may be followed by a relay to first base (interference by R3 is a consideration). If the first play develops at any other base, *stay home*. Observe the action; rule immediately if there is interference by B1; prepare to cover third base in the event of a subsequent play.

6. Offer your opinion of a swipe tag or pulled foot at first or third base only if U1 requests help.

7. Realize you have responsibility for any play that develops at home plate.

Notes

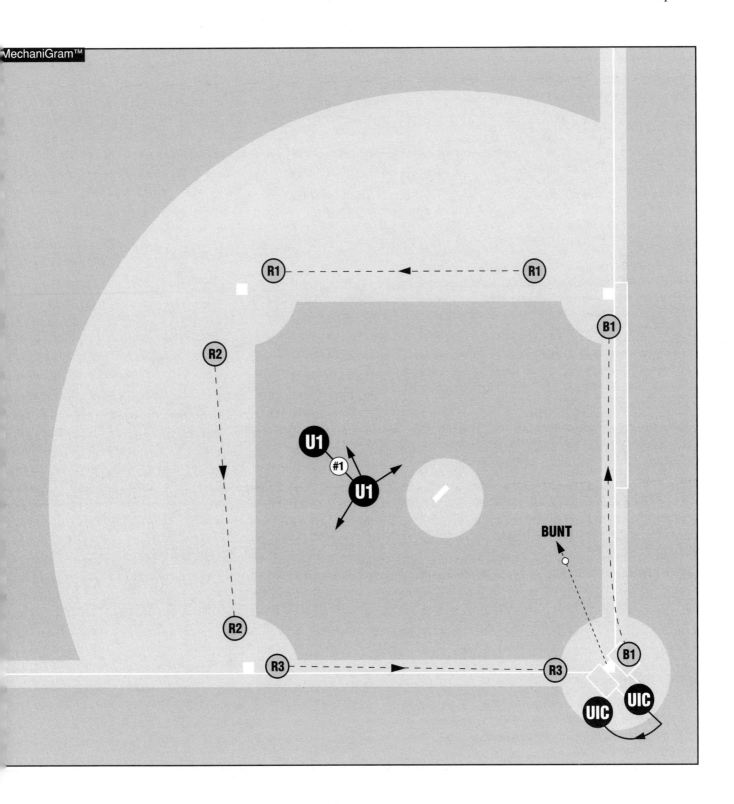

Review: Bases loaded

Base umpire
- Start in position C.
- Adjust back, unless limited by the defensive positioning (is F3 holding the runner?).
- Fair/foul: You have no responsibility.
- Field coverage: You have the "V," beginning with any ball hit directly to F7 and ending with any ball hit directly to F9.
- On the bases: You have all plays at first, second and third base.
- Priorities:
    1. A balk or illegal pitch by the pitcher.
    2. Help for the plate umpire on the half-swing.
    3. A pickoff attempt by the pitcher or catcher.
    4. A "trouble ball" in your area of the outfield — the "V," beginning with any ball hit directly to F7 and ending with any ball hit directly to F9.
    5. A ground ball play — multiple possibilities.
    6. A batted or bunted ball with F3, F1 and B1 all converging at the base.
    7. A clean hit, or any batted ball to your area of the outfield.
    8. An infield fly.

Umpire in chief
- Your first concern is always the pitch: strike or ball.
- Fair/foul: You have all fair/foul decisions.
- Field coverage: You have balls hit to the outfield to the left or right of the "V."
- On the bases: Stay home; you have all plays at home plate and no responsibility for plays at the bases.
- Priorities:
    1. A balk or illegal pitch.
    2. The pitch: ball or strike.
    3. Check-swings and defensive appeals.
    4. A fair/foul call down either foul line.
    5. A "trouble" ball in your area of the outfield: cover the batted ball and return to the plate for a developing play.
    6. A bunted ball when opponents converge — interference/obstruction.
    7. An infield fly.

Quiz
Without referring back, you should be able to answer the following true-false questions. Remember: R1 is always the runner who begins a play at first base; R2 at second; R3 at third; B1 is the batter-runner; fielders are identified by their scoring abbreviations (F1 is the pitcher, F2 the catcher, etc.).

1. If a batted ball lands near the right-field-foul line beyond first base, U1 has the fair/foul decision.
2. UIC will rule immediately if B1 is guilty of interference with a play at first base.
3. UIC always has responsibility for R3 tagging up at third.
4. If UIC follows an errant throw near a dead-ball area, U1 must rotate and cover a play at home plate.
5. Because he is stationed in the middle of the infield, U1 cannot help the plate umpire on a check-swing by B1.
6. When a fly ball is in U1's coverage area, UIC will move toward the third-base dugout to observe simultaneously the catch and R3 tagging up.

ANSWERS: 1-False, 2-True, 3-True, 4-False, 5-False, 6-True

Runner configuration: Runners at first and third

Base umpire position: Position C.

Adjustment factors:

Game situation: Start a bit deeper to open your field of view, but realize that a deep position C sacrifices some of your angle on a pickoff throw to first base.

Defensive tendencies: A pickoff throw to *either* first or third by the pitcher is likely. In addition, aggressive catchers like to throw behind the runner at first and they *love* to pick a runner off third. If the defense has a reputation for unusual plays or the catcher is unusually aggressive, you may adjust forward a step or two "automatically" as a pitch passes the batter. That will make it easier for you to open the angle when a throw to first does occur (your angle to third is already established).

The runner at first: When the players are young or less developed, only the slowest runners will not steal; as the players grow and develop, fewer runners steal "automatically."

The batter: Simply for your personal safety, if B1 is a strong, right-handed pull hitter, you might consider adjusting back a step. That will give you more time to react to a ball batted in your direction.

In order of importance, be prepared for the following situations:
1. A balk or illegal pitch.
2. Pick off attempt at first base by the pitcher.
3. Pick off attempt at third base by the pitcher.
4. Help for the plate umpire on the check-swing.
5. Pick off attempt at first base by the catcher.
6. A second-base steal and the accompanying "trick" plays.
7. Pickoff attempt at third base by the catcher.
8. A "trouble" ball in your area of the outfield — the "V," beginning with any ball hit directly to F7 and ending with any ball hit directly to F9.
9. A ground ball in the infield: You have all plays at first and second; UIC will assist on a play at third after R3 scores. UIC has responsibility for any play that develops at home plate.
10. A batted or bunted ball with F1, F3, F4 and/or B1 converging at the base.

Plate umpire anticipation:

Your initial position is always behind the plate. As the pitcher begins his delivery, come set in your stance. Your initial responsibility is always calling the pitch a strike or a ball. Respond to the batted ball and the action as it develops.

Batted ball in the infield: Determine fair/foul as appropriate. U1 will always rule on the first play in the infield; you have complete responsibility for any play at home plate. In the event of a double-play opportunity, observe the action at second base and be prepared to assist with a pulled foot or swipe tag at first base; cover dead-ball areas in case of an errant throw.

Batted ball to the outfield: You have the areas from F7 to the left-field dead-ball area and from F9 to the right-field dead-ball area. *Stay home!* You must see R3 touch the plate. To right field: Take a position on the first-base line extended; rule fair/foul and catch/no catch as necessary. To left field: Take a position on the third-base line extended; rule fair/foul, catch/no catch as necessary. If R3 scores unchallenged on a batted ball to the outfield, you will assist U1 by covering third base (if R1 attempts to advance from first to third) — *Communicate!*

In order of importance, be prepared for the following situations:
1. A balk or illegal pitch.
2. The pitch: ball or strike.
3. Check-swings and defensive appeals.
4. A fair/foul call down either foul line.
5. A tag play on R3 trying to score.
6. A "trouble" ball in your area of the outfield.
7. A subsequent play on R1 at third base.
8. A double-play ball in the infield — observe and support U1.
9. A bunted ball when opponents converge — interference/obstruction.

Case Study 41 — Pickoff throw to first

Game situation: Runners at first and third

Action on the field: Pitcher or catcher attempts pickoff at first base

RESPONSIBILITIES

Base umpire

1. Read the pitcher's throw to first base OR the catcher's throw after the pitch.

2. Step directly forward toward home plate. Ideally you will step with your right foot, then your left foot, then pivot on your left foot as you take a final step with your right foot and turn to observe the play. (At a minimum, step left, pivot and turn as you step right.) The steps will open your angle to view the play. For a catcher's pickoff: Follow the same path, but the catcher's slower release and longer throw should allow you to take at least two additional steps.

3. Set. Observe the play. *Timing!* Do not rule R1 out unless you are certain F3 has complete control of the ball. If the play breaks down due to a bad throw, prepare to lead R1 to second base.

4. Realize that subsequent plays are possible: If R1 breaks for second, you'll have to adjust and move toward the second-base cutout for that play; if F3 throws across the infield, you'll have to turn with the throw and adjust, then set before a play at third occurs.

5. If he is not retired, continue to observe R1 as long as F3 has the ball.

Plate umpire

1. Read the pitcher's move to first OR call the pitch and observe the catcher's throw. Observe the pitcher's entire move to insure there is no balk. Observe the action at home plate — is B1 guilty of interfering with F2's throw?

3. Step back to obtain a clear view of the play at first base; observe the play; glance repeatedly at R3 to determine whether he will try to score.

4. Read the throw. If the throw is errant, stay near home and observe the errant throw to rule on a play near a dead-ball line — you must also observe R3 touching home plate!

Notes

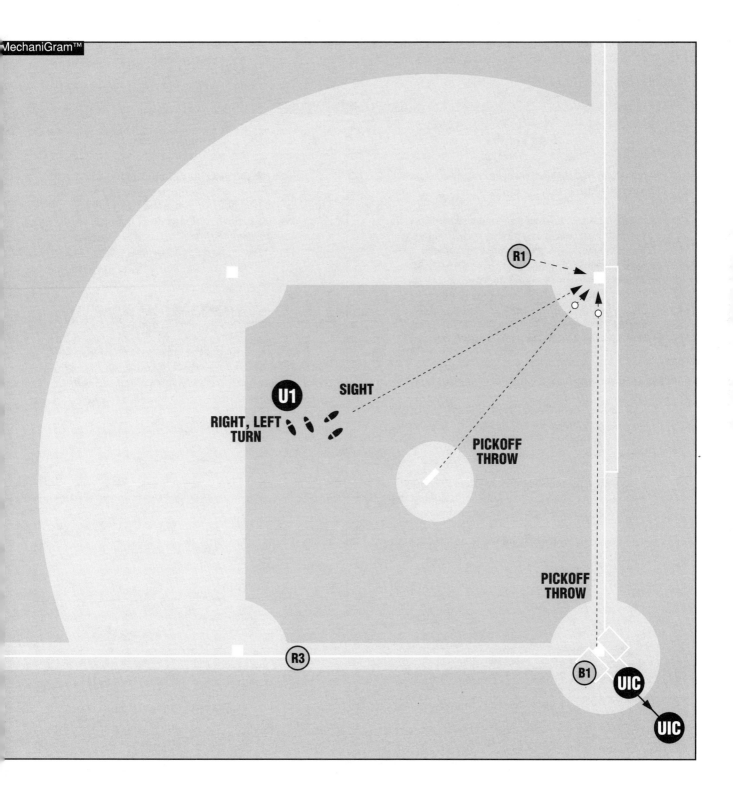

Case Study 42 — Pickoff throw to third

Game situation: Runners at first and third

Action on the field: Pitcher or catcher attempts pickoff at third base

RESPONSIBILITIES

Base umpire

1. Read the pitcher's throw to third base OR the catcher's throw after the pitch.

2. Your angle is somewhat open, so step directly toward third base. For a pitcher's pickoff, move at least two steps (more if your reaction, speed and agility allow); for a catcher's slower release and longer throw, move at least three or four steps (more if your reaction, speed and agility allow).

3. Set. Observe the play. As the play develops, focus on the fielder's glove — it is the slowest moving element and the easiest to observe. If the glove tags the runner before the runner reaches the base, you *may* have an out.

4. *Timing!* Do not rule R3 out unless you are certain F5 has complete control of the ball. If the play breaks down due to a bad throw, prepare to lead R1 to second base.

5. Realize that subsequent plays are possible: If R1 breaks for second, you'll have to adjust and move toward the second-base cutout for that play.

6. If he is not retired, continue to observe R3 as long as F5 has the ball.

Plate umpire

1. Read the pitcher's move to third OR call the pitch and observe the catcher's throw. Observe the pitcher's entire move to insure there is no balk. Observe the action at home plate — is B1 guilty of interfering with F2's throw?

3. Step back to obtain a clear view of the play at third base; observe the play.

4. Read the throw. If the throw is errant, stay near home and observe the errant throw to rule on a play near a dead-ball line — you must also observe R3 touching home plate!

Notes

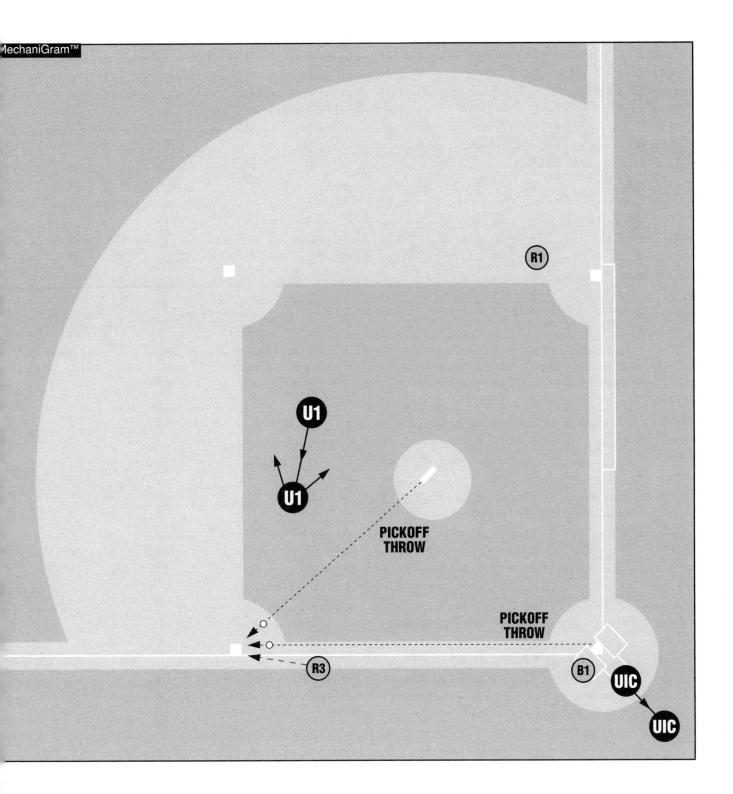

Case Study 43 — Second-base steal

Game situation: Runners at first and third

Action on the field: R1 is stealing

RESPONSIBILITIES

Base umpire	Plate umpire
1. Read the runner's break in your peripheral vision.	1. Call the pitch: ball or strike.
2. Read the catcher. If he throws to third, move aggressively two or three steps toward third base and set; focus on the fielder's glove as the play develops. *Timing!* Do not rule R3 out unless you are certain the fielder has complete control of the ball.	2. Observe the action at home plate — is B1 guilty of interfering with F2's throw?
3. If the catcher throws through to second: Keep your chest to the ball as you turn your shoulders slightly to your left and take one or two cross-over steps toward second. Move toward, but not into the cutout. Be alert: The catcher's throw may be cut off by F1, F4 or F6, which could lead to a play at third base.	5. Read the throw. If the throw is errant, observe R3 touching home plate, then move toward the dead-ball area on the third-base side. If a play at third develops, rule on an overthrow near a dead-ball area.
4. Read the throw and prepare to adjust on a bad throw.	
5. Let the throw turn you toward second base. If the throw is wide toward right field, move closer to second base; on any other bad throw, adjust by moving closer to the direct line between first and second.	
6. Set. Observe the play. *Timing!* Do not rule R1 out unless you are certain the fielder has complete control of the ball. If the play breaks down due to a bad throw, prepare to lead R1 to third base.	
7. If he is not retired, continue to observe R1 as long as the fielder has the ball.	

Notes

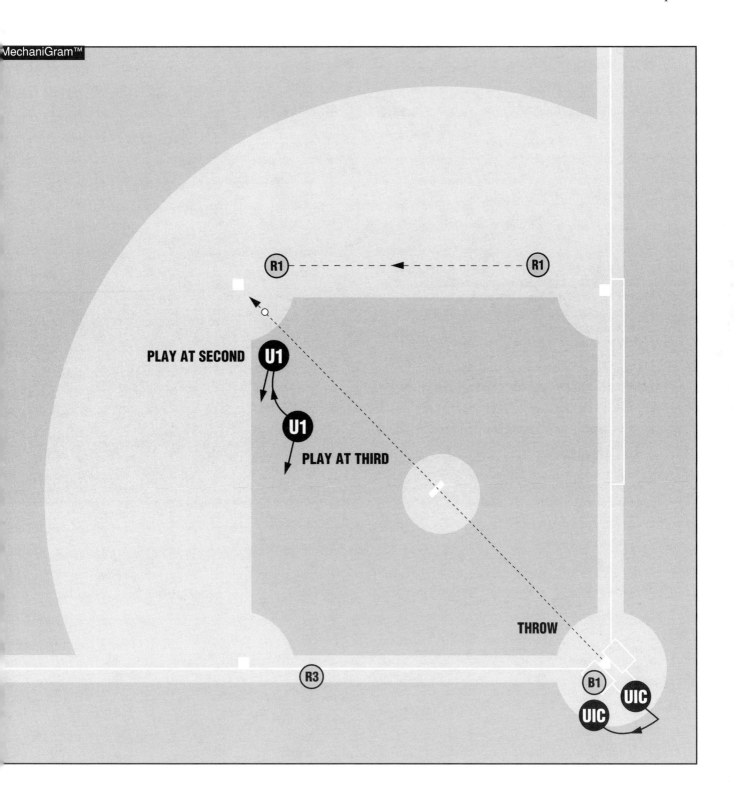

Case Study 44 — Fly ball & Time play

Game situation: Runners at first and third, one out

Action on the field: B1 flies to the middle of the outfield

RESPONSIBILITIES

Base umpire

1. Step up, turn and face the ball; pause, read and react. Read the position of the fielder making the play and determine whether this is a ball in your coverage area (it is) and whether this is a "trouble" ball (it is not).

2. Since it is not a "trouble" ball: Move back two or three steps toward the pitcher's mound to "open" your field of view. Glance occasionally at R1 to determine whether he is "half way" or tagging. Insure that your position does not hinder the fielder's potential throw to any base.

3. If there is a catch (there is), signal only if the catch is made "below the knee" in your coverage area; verbally inform your partner of a routine catch in your coverage area.

4. After the catch: You have tag-up responsibility at first base *and* any play that develops on R1; you would also have a play on R3 at third in a case of very poor base running. Keep your chest to the ball and let the throw take you to the next play. Establish your set position before the play occurs. *Timing!*

5. If R1 is retired for the third out, is it imperative that you signal promptly — UIC will respond by immediately ruling whether R3 scores.

6. If a runner remains on base, observe the runner whenever the ball is near his location.

Plate umpire

1. Pause, read and react. Read the developing play and your partner.

2. If fair/foul is a consideration, assume a position on the foul line extended, set before the play occurs and rule fair/foul and catch/no catch as necessary. You are responsible for R3 tagging up at third.

3. If the ball is in U1's coverage area, move toward the third-base dugout and open your field of view. You must observe the catch and R3's tag-up at third base.

4. After the catch: You have responsibility for any play that develops at home plate. *Timing!*

5. If a subsequent play develops on R1, you must determine whether R3 scores before R1 is retired. Assume a position on foul ground near home plate. Your position must allow you to see R3 scoring *and* the developing play on R1. If U1 declares out R1, you must *immediately* determine and announce whether R3 scored before the third out.

Notes

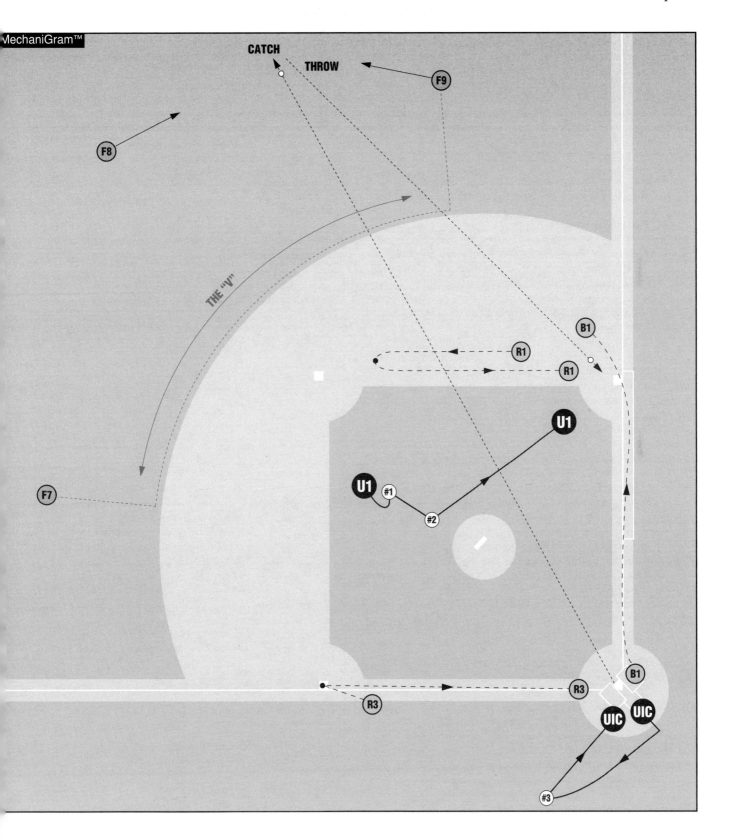

Case Study 45 — Ground ball to the base umpire's right

Game situation: Runners at first and third

Action on the field: B1 hits ground ball played by F5 or F6

RESPONSIBILITIES

Base umpire	Plate umpire
1. Step up, turn and face the ball. Read ground ball and possible double play.	1. Pause, read and react. Read the possible double-play ball.
2. Realize there is always the possibility of a play at third base, either as the first play or as a subsequent play on a "surprise" throw. You have all plays at first, second and third until R3 scores and UIC informs you that he will cover a subsequent play on R1 at third base.	2. Clear the catcher; if the ball is hit near the third-base line, straddle the line and observe the play. You must first rule fair or foul.
3. If the batted ball is fielded cleanly (it is), prepare for a double-play attempt.	3. If fair/foul is not a concern, move a few feet toward third, but *stay home*.
4. As the infielder prepares to make the first throw, move one or two steps toward first base (anticipating a double-play relay) while you keep your chest to the ball. Let the infielder's throw to second base turn your shoulders square to the bag. Set. *Determine safe/out of R1.* (*Timing!* Do not rule R1 out unless the fielder has complete control of the ball.)	4. You are responsible for any play that develops on R3 at home plate.
5. If there is no relay or the relay goes to home plate, stop and move one or two steps directly toward second base, and declare R1 out or safe. If the subsequent play goes to third (extremely rare), *declare* R1 out or safe as you move toward third base. If the relay throw is going to first (it is), turn slightly (chest to right field or the right field corner); observe the remaining action at second base as you move toward the first base line (as far as the play will allow, usually two or three steps) and prepare for the relay to first. *Declare* R1 out or safe, aloud, *while moving* toward the first base line.	7. If a subsequent play develops at first base, observe. Be prepared to rule on interference by B1 or an overthrow; offer your opinion of a swipe tag or pulled foot only if U1 requests help. If R3 scores and a subsequent play develops on R1 advancing to third base, you should be able to cover that play — *communicate!*
6. Let the relay throw turn you toward first base. (The play at first will happen very quickly, so be prepared.)	NOTE: If R1 is safe at second, after R3 scores you may be able to assist on a subsequent play at third.
7. Set for the play at first and observe the play. *Timing!* Do not rule B1 out unless the fielder has complete control of the ball.	
8. When the play is over, if a runner remains on base, observe the runner whenever the ball is near his location.	
NOTE: Proper timing on the turn to first will keep your eyes on the ball until the fielder makes the relay throw. If the play breaks down (dropped ball, errant throw, interference at second) move directly to second base and "sell" your out or safe decision with an emphatic voice-and-signal combination.	

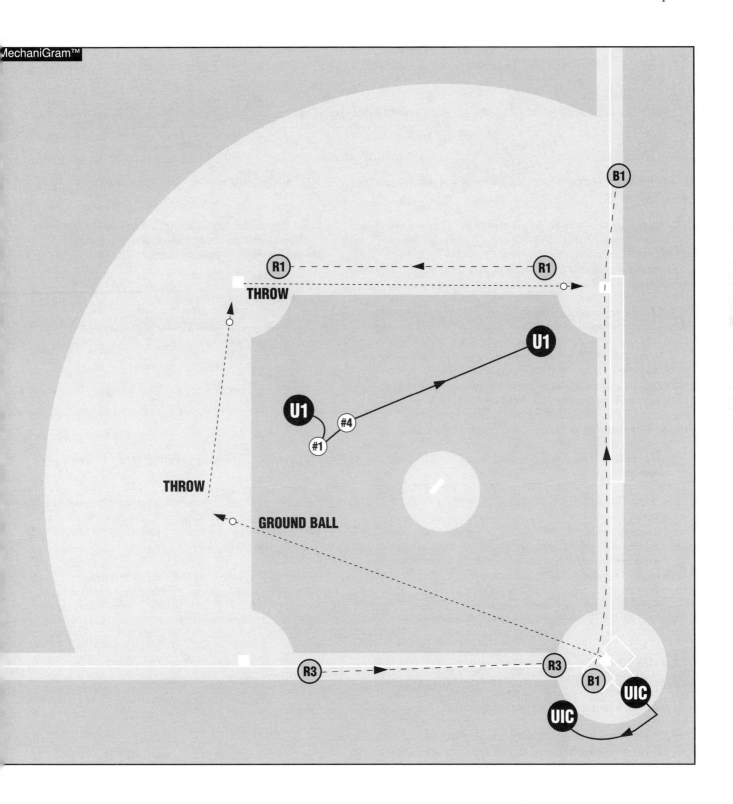

Case Study 46 — Ground ball to the base umpire's left

Game situation: Runners at first and third

Action on the field: B1 hits ground ball played by F1, F3 or F4

RESPONSIBILITIES

Base umpire

1. Step up, turn and face the ball. Read ground ball and possible double play.

2. Realize the possibility of a play at third base exists, but is diminished if F3 or F4 field the batted ball. You have all plays at first, second and third until R3 scores and UIC informs you that he will cover a subsequent play on R1 at third base.

3. If the batted ball is fielded cleanly (it is), prepare for a double-play attempt.

4. As the infielder prepares to make the first throw, move one or two steps toward the 45-foot line (anticipating a double-play relay) while you keep your chest to the ball. Insure that your position does not hinder the fielder's potential throw to any base. Let the infielder's throw to second base turn your shoulders square to the bag. Set. *Determine* safe/out of R1. (*Timing!* Do not rule R1 out unless the fielder has complete control of the ball.)

5. Turn slightly (chest to right field or the right-field corner); observe the remaining action at second base as you move toward the first base line (as far as the play will allow, usually two or three steps) and prepare for the relay to first. *Declare* R1 out or safe, aloud, *while moving* toward the first base line.

6. Let the relay throw turn you toward first base. (The play at first will happen very quickly, so be prepared.)

7. Set. Observe the play. *Timing!* Do not rule B1 out unless the fielder has complete control of the ball.

8. When the play is over, if a runner remains on base, observe the runner whenever the ball is near his location.

NOTE: Proper timing on the turn to first will keep your eyes on the ball until the fielder makes the relay throw. If the play breaks down (dropped ball, errant throw, interference at second) move directly to second base and "sell" your out or safe decision with an emphatic voice-and-signal combination.

Plate umpire

1. Pause, read and react. Read the possible double-play ball.

2. Clear the catcher; if the ball is hit near the first-base line, straddle the foul line extended and observe the play. You must first rule fair or foul.

3. If fair/foul is not a concern, move a few feet toward third base, but *stay home*.

4. You are responsible for any play that develops on R3 at home plate.

7. If a subsequent play develops at first base, observe. Be prepared to rule on interference by B1 or an overthrow; offer your opinion of a swipe tag or pulled foot only if U1 requests help. If R3 scores and a subsequent play develops on R1 advancing to third base, you should be able to cover that play — *communicate!*

NOTE: If R1 is safe at second, do not return to the plate area. If a play develops at third base after R3 scores, you should be able to move to third base and take the play. *Communicate!*

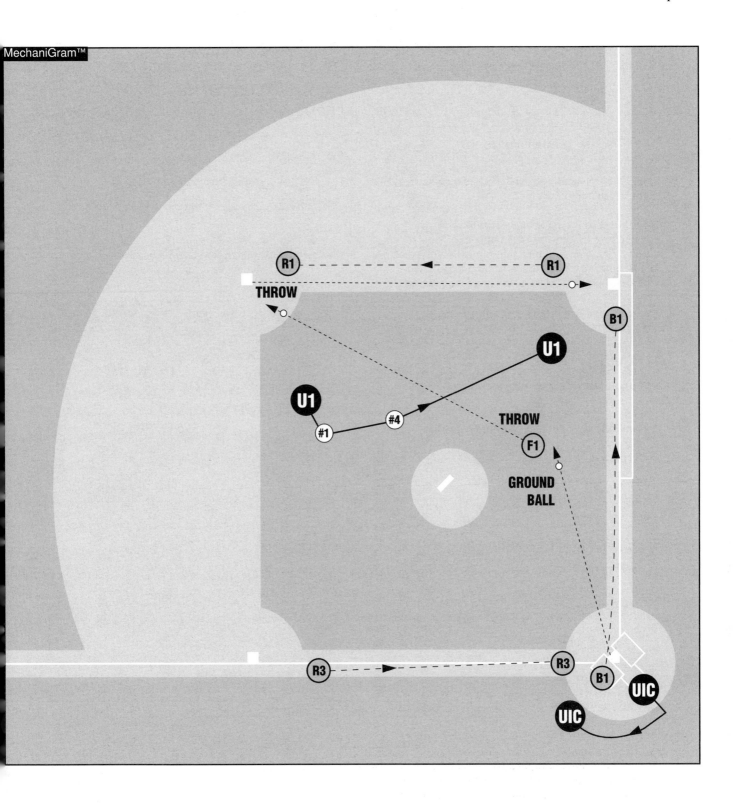

Case Study 47 — Base hit to the outfield

Game situation: Runners at first and third

Action on the field: Clean hit to the outfield

RESPONSIBILITIES

Base umpire	Plate umpire
1. Step up, turn and face the ball; pause, read and react. Read "hit."	1. Pause, read and react. Read "hit."
2. Move back two or three steps toward the pitcher's mound to "open" your field of view.	2. Clear the catcher.
3. Remain aware of the status of the ball as you observe both R1 and B1 advancing to touch bases.	3. If fair/foul is a consideration, assume a position several steps up the foul line, set before the play occurs and rule fair or foul; you also must observe R3 touching home plate.
4. As the ball returns to the infield, you are responsible for plays that develop at first and second. UIC will come up the line and take a play at third base (be alert for his verbal communication). Let the throw lead you to the play, move aggressively into position, and set before the play occurs. *Timing!*	4. In all other cases, remain in foul territory as you move half way up the third-base line; glance back toward home plate to observe R3 touching the plate. After R3 scores, read the developing play. Move farther up the third base line and take any developing play on R1 advancing to third — *communicate!*
5. When runners remain on base, observe carefully whenever the ball is near a runner's location.	

Notes

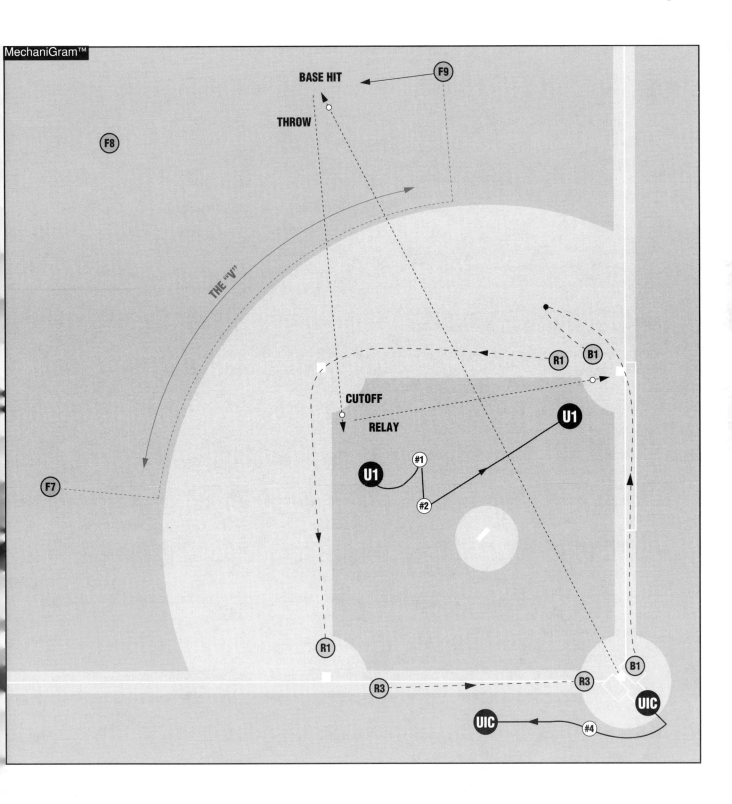

Review: Runners at first and third

Base umpire
• Start in position C.
• Adjust based on the game situation and the players' ability.
• Fair/foul: You have no responsibility.
• Field coverage: You have the "V," beginning with any ball hit directly to F7 and ending with any ball hit directly to F9.
• On the bases: You have all plays at first and second base; UIC will assist on a play at third after R3 scores.
• Priorities:

    1. A balk or illegal pitch.
    2. Pick off attempt at first base by the pitcher.
    3. Pick off attempt at third base by the pitcher.
    4. Help for the plate umpire on the check-swing.
    5. Pick off attempt at first base by the catcher.
    6. A second-base steal and the accompanying "trick" plays.
    7. Pickoff attempt at third base by the catcher.
    8. A "trouble" ball in your area of the outfield — the "V," beginning with any ball hit directly to F7 and ending with any ball hit directly to F9.
    9. A ground ball in the infield: You have all plays at first and second base. UIC has responsibility for all plays on R1 at third base and all plays that develop at home.
    10. A batted or bunted ball with F1, F3, F4 and/or B1 converging at the base.

Umpire in chief
• Your first concern is always the pitch: strike or ball.
• Fair/foul: You have all fair/foul decisions.
• Field coverage: You have balls hit to the outfield to the left or right of the "V."
• On the bases: You have all plays at home plat.e. After R3 scores cover a play at third base.
• Priorities:

    1. A balk or illegal pitch.
    2. The pitch: ball or strike.
    3. Check-swings and defensive appeals.
    4. A fair/foul call down either foul line.
    5. A tag play on R3 trying to score.
    6. A "trouble" ball in your area of the outfield.
    7. A subsequent play on R1 at third base.
    8. A double-play ball in the infield — observe and support U1.
    9. A bunted ball when opponents converge — interference/obstruction.

Quiz
Without referring back, you should be able to answer the following true-false questions. Remember: R1 is always the runner who begins a play at first base; R2 at second; R3 at third; B1 is the batter-runner; fielders are identified by their scoring abbreviations (F1 is the pitcher, F2 the catcher, etc.).

1. If B1 grounds to the left side, UIC will move out in front of the plate to observe the play at second base.
2. On a fly ball down the right-field line, UIC has fair/foul, catch/no catch and R3 tagging up at third.
3. To cover the first part of a double play, U1 will move toward the second-base cutout.
4. To cover the second part of a double play, U1 will move toward the first-base cutout.
5. After R3 scores on a hit to the outfield, UIC will cover R1 advancing to third base.
6. On a "trouble" ball in the "V," U1 will determine catch/no catch from a position on the infield grass.

Runner configuration: Runner at second

Base umpire position: Position C.

Adjustment factors: Frequently, in position C you will obstruct the runner's or shortstop's view of the pitcher or the plate. Before a player asks you to move, decide whether you are going to move (you normally should) and in what direction. Also, realize that moving forward or back a step alters your position in the player's view. Even if someone asks you to move "right," you might be better off moving slightly left and a half-step forward or back.

Game situation: Is a bunt in order? Adjust forward a step or two. When a bunt does occur, it will be easier to move into position and prepare for a play at either first or third base; if the bunt is missed and a throw goes to second, you will have plenty of time to move toward the second-base cutout. Is the game one-sided? That means conservative base running, few steals and almost no bunting, so you can move back one or two steps from your normal position. That will make it easier to turn, set and adjust if the pitcher attempts a pickoff.

Defensive tendencies: If the defense has a reputation for unusual plays or the catcher is unusually aggressive, you may adjust forward a step or two. If the defense has a reputation for second-base pickoffs, you may adjust back a step or two and move a step or two closer to the center of the infield. That will give you more time to turn and set, and a better angle for a pickoff play at second.

The runner: If the catcher is at least average for the level of play, third-base steals are rare (almost unheard of with no outs or two outs). You may adjust back a step or two. But if R2 is a recognized base stealer or if the situation seems right for a steal, adjust forward from your normal position.

The batter: Simply for your personal safety, if B1 is a strong, right-handed pull hitter, you might consider adjusting back a step. That will give you more time to react to a ball batted in your direction. You'll rarely be hurt by that step because the kind of power hitter we're discussing rarely has a runner steal in front of him. Coaches don't want to "take the bat out of his hand."

In order of importance, be prepared for the following situations:
1. A balk or illegal pitch.
2. Help for the plate umpire on the check-swing.
3. Pick off attempt at second base by the pitcher.
4. A third-base steal — as F1 delivers, glance over your right shoulder to see if R2 is breaking for third.
5. Pickoff attempt at second base by the catcher.
6. A "trouble ball" in your area of the outfield — the "V," beginning with any ball hit directly to F7 and ending with any ball hit directly to F9.
7. A ground ball in the infield: You have all plays at first and second, and primary responsibility for plays at third base; UIC is responsible for any play that develops at home plate and may be able to cover a subsequent play at third base.
8. A batted or bunted ball with F1, F3, F4 and/or B1 converging at the base.
9. A ball hit to the outfield followed by a play on B1 at any base.

Plate umpire anticipation:
Your initial position is always behind the plate. As the pitcher begins his delivery, come set in your stance. Your initial responsibility is always calling the pitch a strike or a ball. Respond to the batted ball and the action as it develops.

Batted ball in the infield: Determine fair/foul as appropriate. U1 will always rule on the first play in the infield; you have primary responsibility for any play at home plate; if the first play is on B1 at first base, you may be able to assist on a subsequent play at third base.

Batted ball to the outfield: You have the areas from F7 to the left-field dead-ball area and from F9 to the right-field dead-ball area. To right field: Trail B1 toward first base; rule fair/foul and catch/no catch as necessary; you are responsible for the lead runner if he tries to advance to home. To left field: Move along the foul line or into the infield and rule fair/foul and catch/no catch as necessary; you are responsible for the lead runner if he tries to advance to third or home.

In order of importance, be prepared for the following situations:
1. A balk or illegal pitch.
2. The pitch: ball or strike.
3. Check-swings and defensive appeals.
4. A fair/foul call down either foul line.
5. A "trouble" ball in your area of the outfield.
6. Any subsequent play on R2 at third base; any play at home.
7. A bunted ball when opponents converge — interference/obstruction.

Case Study 48 — Third-base steal

Game situation: Runner at second

Action on the field: R2 is stealing

RESPONSIBILITIES

Base umpire	Plate umpire
(As F1 delivers, glance over your right shoulder to see if R2 is stealing.)	1. Call the pitch: ball or strike.
1. Read the runner's break in your peripheral vision.	2. Observe the action at home plate — is B1 guilty of interfering with F2's throw?
2. As soon as the pitch clears the batter, move aggressively toward the mid-point of the third-base line (half way between home and third). This will open the angle and give you a better view of the tag play at third. You want to establish a 90-degree angle between your line of sight and the runner's path to third base.	3. Read the throw. If the throw is errant, prepare to move toward the dead-ball area on the third-base side. You are responsible for any play that develops at home plate.
3. Let the throw turn you toward third base, set and observe the play.	
NOTE: A third-base steal is among the most difficult plays for a two-man crew. Here's a hint: As you look to third, focus on the fielder's glove (instead of looking for the ball) and determine whether the glove tags the runner before the runner touches the base. If the tag is in time, wait to see the ball in the glove before you declare the runner out.	
4. *Timing!* Do not rule R1 out unless you are certain the fielder has complete control of the ball.	
5. If he is not retired, continue to observe R2 as long as the fielder has the ball.	

Notes

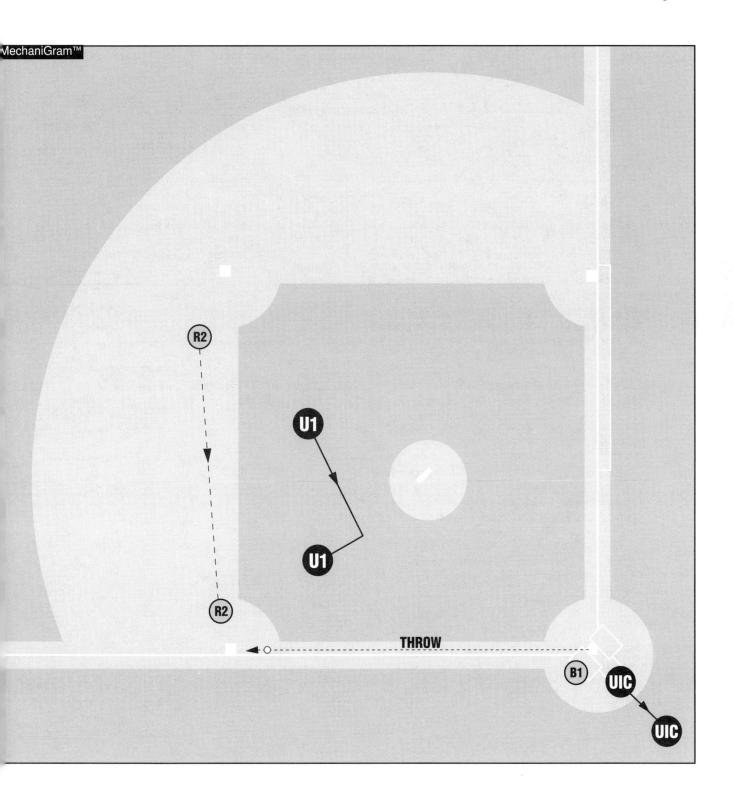

Case Study 49 — Fly ball in the "V"

Game situation: Runner at second

Action on the field: B1 flies to the middle of the outfield

RESPONSIBILITIES

Base umpire	Plate umpire
(As F1 delivers, glance over your right shoulder to see if R2 is stealing.)	1. Pause, read and react. Read the developing play and your partner.
1. Step up, turn and face the ball; pause, read and react. Read the position of the fielder making the play and determine whether this is a ball in your coverage area (it is) and whether this is a "trouble" ball (it is).	2. With the ball in U1's coverage area, move half way up the third-base line in foul territory to observe the play. If R2 is tagging, move at least half-way to third base.
2. If you read a "trouble" ball, move toward the coming play, but only to the edge of the infield grass. ***Do not leave the infield grass!*** If it is not a "trouble" ball, move back two or three steps toward the pitcher's mound to "open" your field of view.	4. After the catch: You have responsibility for any play that develops on R2 at third base and for any play that develops at home plate. If R2 commits to third, continue moving up the line and read the throw. If the throw is to third and a play develops, move into fair territory at the third-base cutout; establish your set position before the play occurs. *Timing!*
3. If there is a catch (there is), signal only if the catch is made "below the knee"; verbally inform your partner of a routine catch. If a difficult play results in no catch, signal "safe" and verbally call, "No catch! No catch!"	
4. After the catch: You have tag-up responsibility at second base. If R2 advances to third, the plate umpire has responsibility for the play; you have the play at second if R2 starts to third and returns. Establish your set position before the play occurs. *Timing!*	5. If R2 advances safely to third and the play ends, clear the runner before returning to home plate.
5. If R2 remains on base, observe the runner whenever the ball is near his location.	

Notes

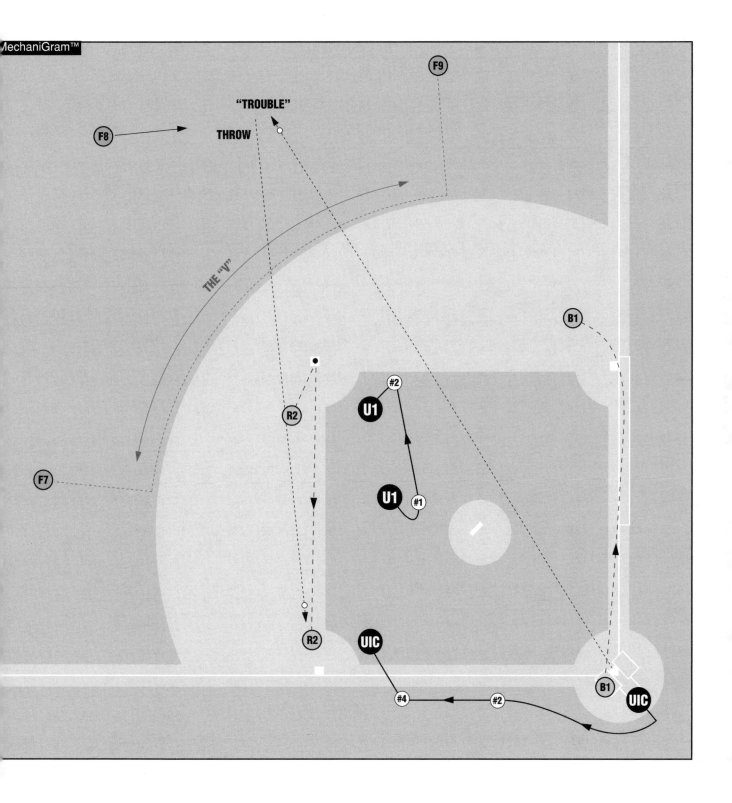

Case Study 50 — Fly ball to left field

Game situation: Runner at second base

Action on the field: Left fielder moves toward the line on a fly ball

RESPONSIBILITIES

Base umpire	Plate umpire
(As F1 delivers, glance over your right shoulder to see if R2 is stealing.)	1. Pause, read and react. Read the position of the fielder making the play and determine whether this is a ball in your coverage area (it is) and whether this is a "trouble" ball.
1. Step up, turn and face the ball; pause, read and react. Read the position of the fielder making the play and determine whether this is a ball in your coverage area (it is not).	2. Since the ball is in your coverage area, clear the catcher and move about half way up the third-base line and communicate with your partner: "I've got the ball!"
2. Since the ball is not in your area: Move back two or three steps toward the pitcher's mound to "open" your field of view. Remain aware of the fly ball status as you observe both R2, if he is tagging up, and B1. Listen for your partner to inform you of a catch.	3. If fair/foul is a consideration, move aggressively along the third-base line, set before the play occurs and rule fair or foul.
	4. Develop the best angle possible to observe the catch/no catch.
	5. If there is a catch (there is), signal only if the catch is made "below the knee"; verbally inform your partner of any catch: "Bill, that's a catch." If the ball is a hit, you are responsible for R2 advancing to third base and potentially to home plate.
6. After the catch: You have tag-up responsibility at second base and a play there if R2 starts toward third and returns. Establish your set position before the play occurs. *Timing!*	6. After the catch: Read the outfielder's throw. If the throw and R2 approach third and a play develops, move into fair territory at the third-base cutout and establish your set position before the play occurs. *Timing!*
7. If R2 remains on base, observe R2 whenever the ball is near his location.	7. If R2 advances and remains on base, clear the runner before returning to your position behind the plate.

Notes

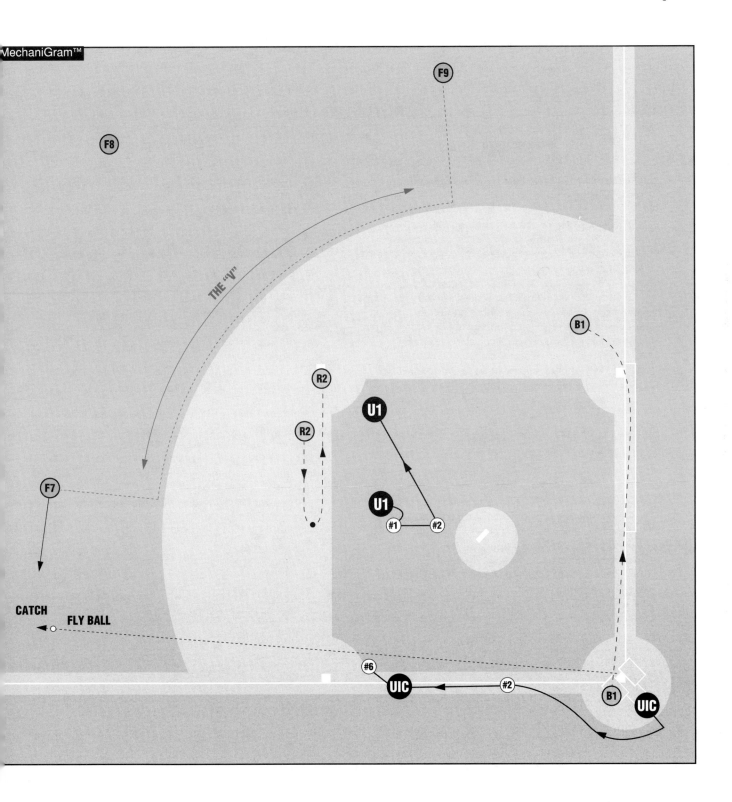

Case Study 51 — Fly ball to right field

Game situation: Runner at second base

Action on the field: Right fielder moves toward the line on a fly ball

RESPONSIBILITIES

Base umpire

(As F1 delivers, glance over your right shoulder to see if R2 is stealing.)

1. Step up, turn and face the ball; pause, read and react. Read the position of the fielder making the play and determine whether this is a ball in your coverage area (it is not).

2. Since the ball is not in your area: Move back two or three steps toward the pitcher's mound to "open" your field of view. Expect your partner to communicate — he should be on the line for the fair/foul and catch/no catch decisions. With your partner on the line, prepare to take R2 into third base after the catch. Remain aware of the fly ball status as you observe both R2 and B1. Listen for your partner to inform you of a catch.

6. After the catch: You have tag-up responsibility at second base and any play that develops on R2 at second or third. If R2 is tagging to advance, move toward the third-base cutout as you read the throw — but do not over-commit! If R2 advances part way to third and returns to second, you have the play at second. Establish your set position before the play occurs. *Timing!*

7. If R2 remains on base, observe R2 whenever the ball is near his location.

Plate umpire

1. Pause, read and react. Read the position of the fielder making the play and determine whether this is a ball in your coverage area (it is).

2. Since the ball is in your coverage area, clear the catcher and move about half way up the first-base line and communicate with your partner: "I'm on the line!"

3. If fair/foul is a consideration, move aggressively along the first-base line, set before the play occurs and rule fair or foul.

4. Develop the best angle possible to observe the catch/no catch.

5. If there is a catch (there is), signal only if the catch is made "below the knee"; verbally inform your partner: "Bill, that's a catch." If the ball is a hit, you are responsible for out-of-play areas and for any play that develops at home plate.

6. After the catch: Return immediately to home plate. You have any play that develops there.

Notes

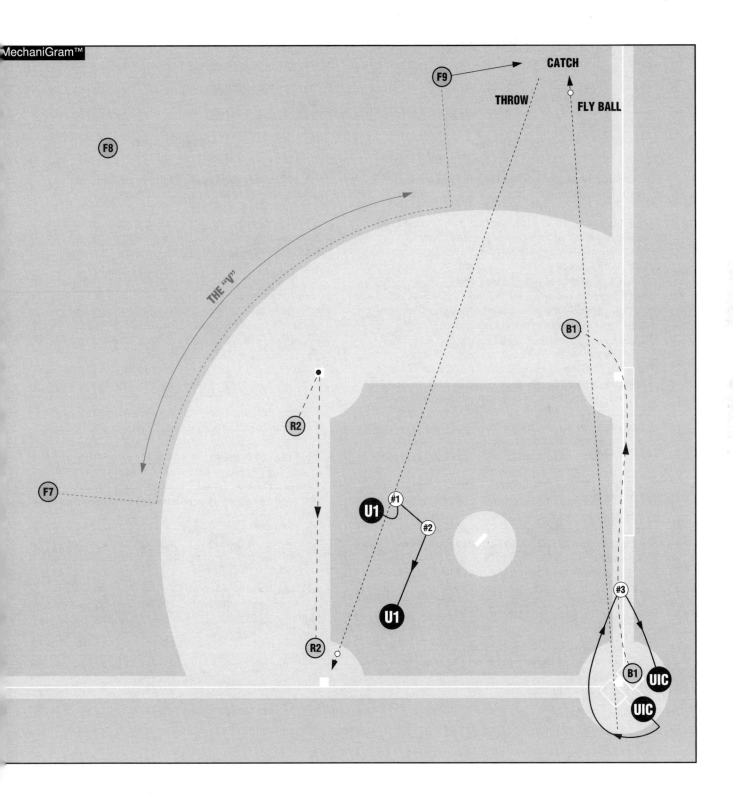

Case Study 52 — Ground ball in the infield

Game situation: Runner at second

Action on the field: B1 hits ground ball played in the infield

RESPONSIBILITIES

Base umpire

(As F1 delivers, glance over your right shoulder to see if R2 is stealing.)

1. Step up, turn and face the ball. Read ground ball and determine where the first play will occur.

2. Realize there is always the possibility of a play at third base, either as the first play or as a subsequent play. You are responsible for the first play that occurs at first, second or third, and for any subsequent play that occurs at first or second base.

3. The first play is generally at first base, but any infielder *could* play on R2 instead of B1. Keep your chest to the ball. Let the infielder's throw turn you to the play. If the first play develops at first base, move several steps across the infield behind the mound and establish the best angle possible for the play at first; if the first play is at second or third, move toward the cutout. In either case, establish your set position before the play occurs.

4. *Timing!* Do not rule a runner out unless the fielder has complete control of the ball. Immediately after an out at first base, take several quick, cross-over steps toward R2 (at second or third) anticipating a subsequent play.

7. When the play is over, if a runner remains on base, observe the runner whenever the ball is near his location.

Plate umpire

1. Pause, read and react. Read ground ball and determine where the first play will occur.

2. Clear the catcher; if the ball is hit near either foul line, straddle the line and observe the play. You must first rule fair or foul.

3. If fair/foul is not a concern, move 10 to 15 feet toward third and prepare to cover a subsequent play at third base. Observe the first play at first base: Be prepared to rule on interference by B1 or an overthrow; offer your opinion of a swipe tag or pulled foot only if U1 requests help.

4. If on a throw to first base R2 breaks for third, move aggressively toward third base but remain in foul territory. Read the play at first and, if there is a subsequent throw to third, read the throw.

5. If the subsequent throw and R2 approach third and a play develops, move into fair territory at the third-base cutout, let the throw turn you to the play and establish your set position before the play occurs. *Timing!*

6. You are responsible for any play that develops at home plate.

7. If R2 advances and remains on base, clear the runner before returning to your position behind the plate.

Notes

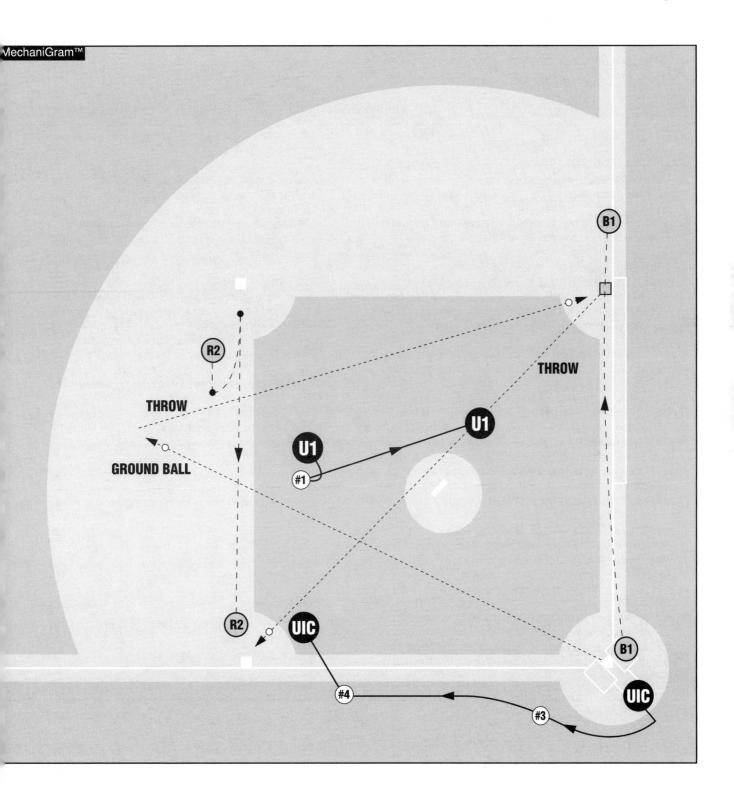

Case Study 53 — Bunt

Game situation: Runner at second

Action on the field: B1 bunts

RESPONSIBILITIES

Base umpire	Plate umpire
(As F1 delivers, glance over your right shoulder to see if R2 is stealing.)	1. Pause, read and react. Read the bunted ball, usually in "the box."
1. Step up, turn and face the ball; pause, read and react. Read the bunted ball, usually in "the box."	2. Clear the catcher; rule fair or foul as necessary.
2. Read whether the play will develop at first or third base; react by moving aggressively two or three steps toward the play. In any event, you have responsibility for the first play and for any subsequent play that develops at first, second or third.	4. Move out to the catcher's left; read the throw and whether the play is at first or third base. *Stay home!*
3. Move to establish a 90-degree angle to the expected throw.	5. On a play at first base, observe the action and rule immediately if there is interference by B1.
4. Read the throw. On a good throw, come to your set position and focus on the play; on a bad throw, adjust to a position which will afford the best possible view of the play. For a play at first base, you'll move across the infield behind the mound, then try to move closer to the 45-foot line (if time permits); for a play at third, you'll move toward the mid-point of the third-base line; for a play at second, move toward the second-base cutout.	6. Offer your opinion of a swipe tag or pulled foot at first base only if U1 requests help.
	7. Realize you have prime responsibility for any play that develops at home plate.
5. *Timing!* Do not rule the runner out unless you are certain the fielder has complete control of the ball. If the play breaks down and you are uncertain of a tag or pulled foot, decide whether your partner may be able to assist. If the play is at first base, communicate with UIC *before* you rule B1 safe or out.	
7. No matter where the first play develops, recognize the possibility of a subsequent play. Immediately after an out at first base, take several quick, cross-over steps toward R2 (at second or third) anticipating a subsequent play.	

Notes

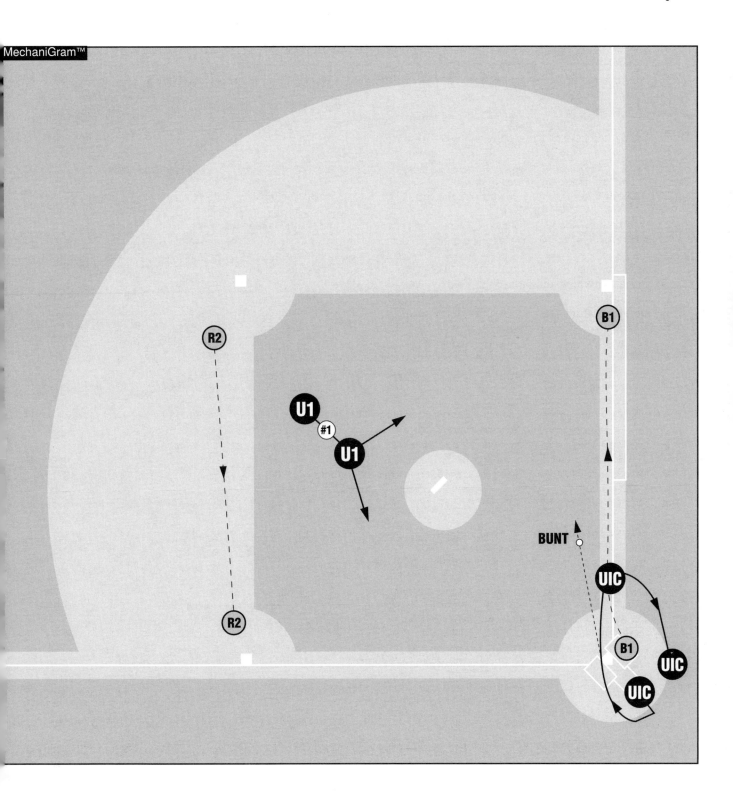

Review: Runner at second

Base umpire
- Start in position C.
- Adjust based on the game situation, the catcher's ability and the runner's speed.
- Fair/foul: You have no responsibility.
- Field coverage: You have the "V," beginning with any ball hit directly to F7 and ending with any ball hit directly to F9.
- On the bases: You have all plays at first, second and third; UIC may be able to cover a subsequent play at third base.
- Priorities:
    1. A balk or illegal pitch.
    2. Help for the plate umpire on the check-swing.
    3. Pick off attempt at second base by the pitcher.
    4. A third-base steal — as F1 delivers, glance over your right shoulder to see if R2 is breaking for third.
    5. Pickoff attempt at second base by the catcher.
    6. A "trouble ball" in your area of the outfield — the "V," beginning with any ball hit directly to F7 and ending with any ball hit directly to F9.
    7. A ground ball in the infield: You have all plays at first and second, and primary responsibility for plays at third base; UIC is responsible for any play that develops at home plate and may be able to cover a subsequent play at third base.
    8. A batted or bunted ball with F1, F3, F4 and/or B1 converging at the base.
    9. A ball hit to the outfield followed by a play on B1 at any base.

Umpire in chief
- Your first concern is always the pitch: strike or ball.
- Fair/foul: You have all fair/foul decisions.
- Field coverage: You have balls hit to the outfield to the left or right of the "V."
- On the bases: You have all plays at home plate and may be able to cover a subsequent play at third base.
- Priorities:
    1. A balk or illegal pitch.
    2. The pitch: ball or strike.
    3. Check-swings and defensive appeals.
    4. A fair/foul call down either foul line.
    5. A "trouble" ball in your area of the outfield.
    6. Any subsequent play on R2 at third base; any play at home.
    7. A bunted ball when opponents converge — interference/obstruction.

Quiz
Without referring back, you should be able to answer the following true-false questions. Remember: R1 is always the runner who begins a play at first base; R2 at second; R3 at third; B1 is the batter-runner; fielders are identified by their scoring abbreviations (F1 is the pitcher, F2 the catcher, etc.).

1. On a third-base steal, U1 will move toward the mid-point of the third-base line.
2. On a ground ball, if the first play is at first base UIC may cover third for any subsequent play.
3. If B1 bunts and U1 is uncertain of a swipe tag at first base, he should rule the batter-runner out or safe before asking UIC for help on the play.
4. If R2 steals third and overslides the base, UIC will rule safe or out on the second tag attempt.
5. If B1 flies to deep left field, UIC will cover a play on R2 at third base.

Runner configuration: Runner at third

Base umpire position: Position C, several steps deeper than "normal."

Adjustment factors: (New umpires should work in the basic position. If you have at least three years of field experience, consider the following points and determine whether you want to adjust from your basic position.)

Game situation: Few adjustments are likely or necessary. If at any time there is a tag play at third base, your 90-degree angle is already established. You'll work several steps deeper than normal primarily to avoid being hit by a batted ball. The only other adjustment you may want to make: If the infield is playing at the edge of the grass, your position C location may obstruct the shortstop. In that case, it is reasonable to adjust by moving to a deep position B.

In order of importance, be prepared for the following situations:

1. A balk or illegal pitch.
2. Help for the plate umpire on the check-swing.
3. Pick off attempt at third base by the pitcher or catcher.
4. A "trouble ball" in your area of the outfield — the "V," beginning with any ball hit directly to F7 and ending with any ball hit directly to F9.
5. A ground ball in the infield: You have all plays at first and second, and primary responsibility for plays at third.
6. A batted or bunted ball with F1, F3, F4 and/or B1 converging at the base.
7. A ball hit to the outfield followed by a play on B1 at any base.

Plate umpire anticipation:

Your initial position is always behind the plate. As the pitcher begins his delivery, come set in your stance. Your initial responsibility is always calling the pitch a strike or a ball. Respond to the batted ball and the action as it develops.

Batted ball in the infield: Determine fair/foul as appropriate. U1 will rule on all plays at first and second, and has primary responsibility for plays at third; you are responsible for any play at home plate; when possible, after R3 scores cover a play at third base.

Batted ball to the outfield: You have the areas from F7 to the left-field dead-ball area and from F9 to the right-field dead-ball area. Unless two are out, you must stay home on any batted ball; if fair/foul is a consideration, straddle the foul line extended and make your decision. You are responsible for R3's tag up at third base and for any play at the plate.

In order of importance, be prepared for the following situations:

1. A balk or illegal pitch.
2. The pitch: ball or strike.
3. Check-swings and defensive appeals.
4. A fair/foul call down either foul line.
5. A "trouble" ball in your area of the outfield.
6. Any play at home plate.
7. A bunted ball when opponents converge — interference/obstruction.

Case Study 54 — Stealing home!

Game situation: Runner at third

Action on the field: R3 is stealing the plate

RESPONSIBILITIES

Base umpire	Plate umpire
1. Read the runner's break in your peripheral vision.	1. Concentrate.
2. Remain alert for a batted ball.	2. Determine whether the pitch is a ball or strike.
3. If the ball clears the batter, unless R3 stops and retreats to third you have nothing to do. (It's rare that you can be a spectator, so enjoy it while you can.)	3. Do not attempt to remove your mask; step forward as the catcher moves to apply the tag; observe the action as best you can.
	4. *First* call the pitch; *second* declare R3 safe or out.

Notes

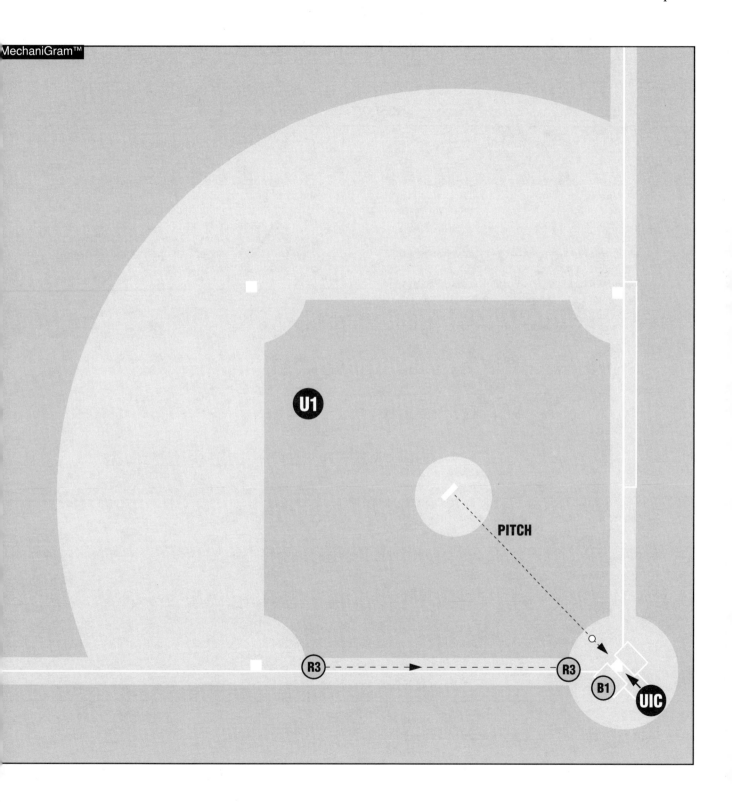

Case Study 55 — Fly ball in the "V"

Game situation: Runner at third

Action on the field: B1 flies to the middle of the outfield

RESPONSIBILITIES

Base umpire

1. Step up, turn and face the ball; pause, read and react. Read the position of the fielder making the play and determine whether this is a ball in your coverage area (it is) and whether this is a "trouble" ball.

2. If you read a "trouble" ball, move toward the coming play, but only to the edge of the infield grass. *Do not leave the infield grass!* If it is not a "trouble" ball, move two or three steps toward the pitcher's mound to "open" your field of view. You must see the catch in the outfield and observe B1 touching first base.

3. If there is a catch (there is), signal only if the catch is made "below the knee"; verbally inform your partner of a routine catch. If a difficult play results in no catch, signal "safe" and verbally call, "No catch! No catch!"

4. After the catch: You are responsible for a play at third base if R3 advances toward the plate and returns. If there is no catch, you are responsible for any play that develops on B1 at first, second or third. Establish your set position before the play occurs. *Timing!*

5. If a runner remains on base, observe the runner whenever the ball is near his location.

Plate umpire

1. Pause, read and react. Read the developing play and your partner.

2. With the ball in U1's coverage area, move toward the third-base dugout to observe the play. This will open your angle and let you observe the fielder's catch and R3 tagging up.

4. After the catch: You have responsibility for any play that develops on R3 at home plate. If R3 tries to score, return to home plate and read the throw. If a play develops at the plate, establish your set position before the play occurs. *Timing!*

Notes

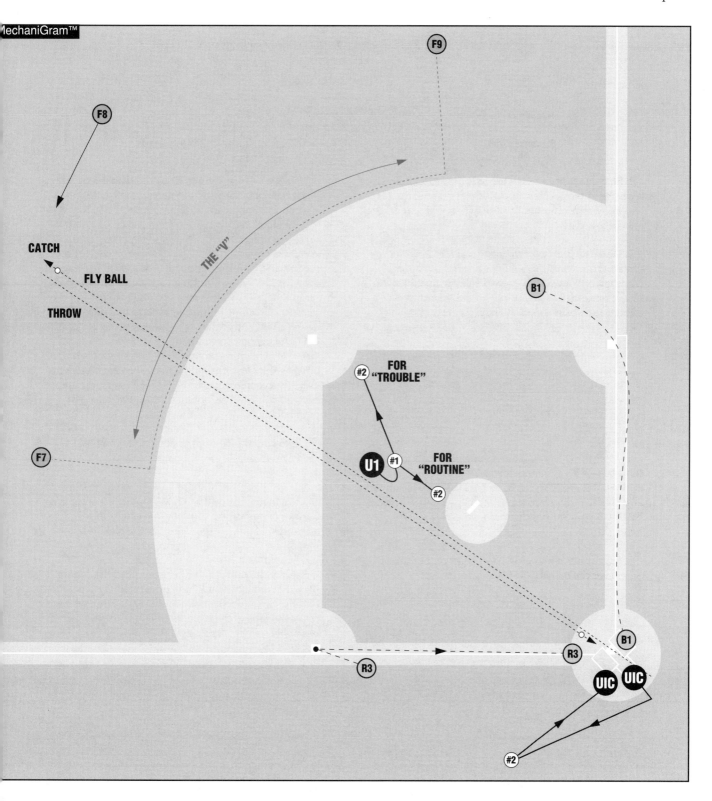

MechaniGram™

F9

F8

CATCH

FLY BALL

THROW

THE "V"

B1

FOR "TROUBLE"
#2

U1 #1

FOR "ROUTINE"
#2

F7

B1

R3

R3

UIC UIC

#2

Case Study 56 — Fly ball to left field

Game situation: Runner at third base

Action on the field: Left fielder moves toward the line on a fly ball

RESPONSIBILITIES

Base umpire

1. Step up, turn and face the ball; pause, read and react. Read the position of the fielder making the play and determine whether this is a ball in your coverage area (it is not).

2. Since the ball is not in your area: Move two or three steps toward the pitcher's mound to "open" your field of view. Remain aware of the fly ball status as you observe B1 touching first base. Listen for your partner to inform you of a catch.

5. After the catch: You are responsible for a play at third base if R3 advances toward the plate and returns. If there is no catch, you are responsible for any play that develops on B1 at first, second or third. Establish your set position before the play occurs. *Timing!*

6. If a runner remains on base, observe the runner whenever the ball is near his location.

Plate umpire

1. Pause, read and react. Read the position of the fielder making the play and determine whether this is a ball in your coverage area (it is) and whether this is a "trouble" ball.

2. Since the ball is in your coverage area, clear the catcher and communicate with your partner: "I've got the ball!" If fair/foul is a consideration or if it is a "trouble" ball, you'll have to establish a position near the third-base line with an unobstructed view of the fielder making the play, but *stay near home!* If fair/foul is not a consideration and it is not a "trouble" ball, move toward the third-base dugout to observe the play. This will open your angle and let you observe the fielder's catch and R3 tagging up. You are responsible for any play that develops at home plate.

3. Develop the best angle possible to observe the catch/no catch.

4. If there is a catch (there is), signal only if the catch is made "below the knee"; verbally inform your partner of any catch: "Bill, that's a catch." If R3 advances, you are responsible for the play at home plate.

5. After the catch: You have responsibility for any play that develops on R3 at home plate. If R3 tries to score, return to home plate and read the throw. If a play develops at the plate, establish your set position before the play occurs. *Timing!*

Notes

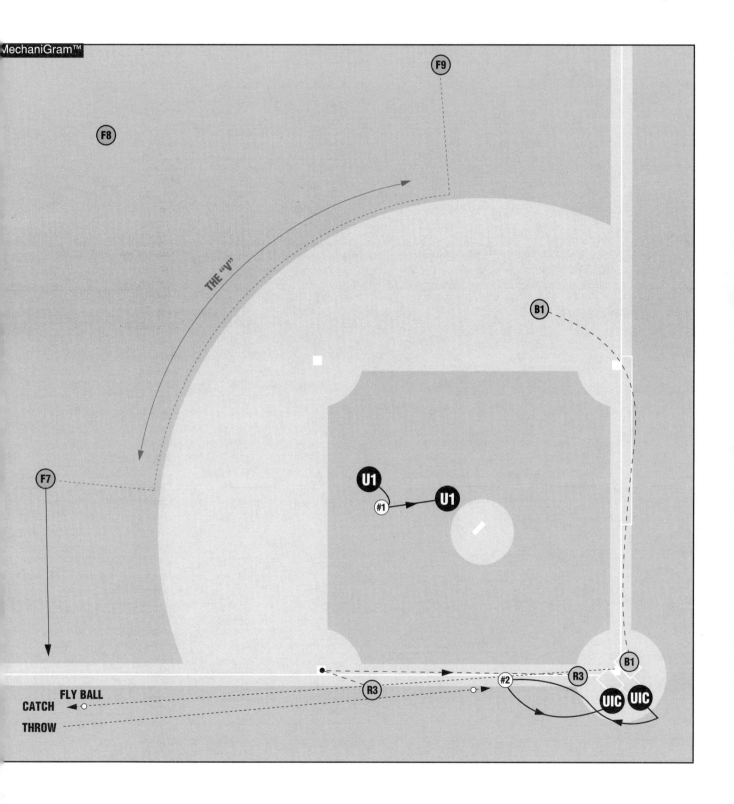

Case Study 57 — Fly ball to right field

Game situation: Runner at third base

Action on the field: Right fielder moves toward the line on a fly ball

RESPONSIBILITIES

Base umpire	Plate umpire
1. Step up, turn and face the ball; pause, read and react. Read the position of the fielder making the play and determine whether this is a ball in your coverage area (it is not).	1. Pause, read and react. Read the position of the fielder making the play and determine whether this is a ball in your coverage area (it is) and whether this is a "trouble" ball.
2. Since the ball is not in your area: Move two or three steps toward the pitcher's mound to "open" your field of view. Remain aware of the fly ball status as you observe B1 touching first base. Listen for your partner to inform you of a catch.	2. Since the ball is in your coverage area, clear the catcher and communicate with your partner: "I'm on the line!" If fair/foul is a consideration or if it is a "trouble" ball, move a short distance up the first-base line to observe the play. You must remain close enough to home plate to return in time to be in position for a play at the plate if R3 tags up or tries to score. Your first priority is the batted ball; after you determine fair/foul and catch/no catch, take a quick glance toward the runner tagging up at third base. It is a difficult look. Remember: Your first priority is the ball! If fair/foul is not a consideration and it is not a "trouble" ball, move toward the third-base dugout to observe the play. This will open your angle and let you observe the fielder's catch and R3 tagging up. You are responsible for any play that develops at home plate.
5. After the catch: You are responsible for a play at third base if R3 advances toward the plate and returns. If there is no catch, you are responsible for any play that develops on B1 at first, second or third. Establish your set position before the play occurs. *Timing!*	3. Develop the best angle possible to observe the catch/no catch.
6. If a runner remains on base, observe the runner whenever the ball is near his location.	4. If there is a catch (there is), signal only if the catch is made "below the knee"; verbally inform your partner of any catch: "Bill, that's a catch." If the ball is a hit, you are responsible for R3 touching home plate.
	5. After the catch: You have responsibility for any play that develops on R3 at home plate. If R3 tries to score, return to home plate and read the throw. If a play develops at the plate, establish your set position before the play occurs. *Timing!*

Notes

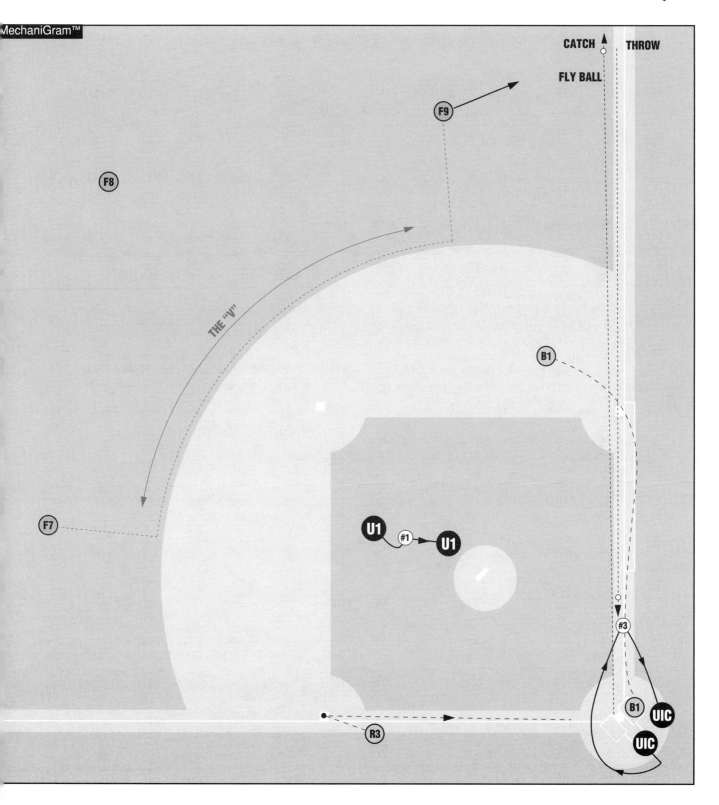

Case Study 58 — Ground ball in the infield

Game situation: Runner at third

Action on the field: B1 hits ground ball played in the infield

RESPONSIBILITIES

Base umpire

1. Step up, turn and face the ball. Read ground ball and determine where the first play will occur.

2. Realize there is always the possibility of a play at third base, and that in most cases the infielder will "look" the runner back to third, then throw to first. You are responsible for the first play that occurs at first or third, and for any subsequent play that occurs at first, second or third base.

3. Keep your chest to the ball. Let the infielder's throw turn you to the play. If the first play develops at first base, move several steps across the infield behind the mound and establish the best angle possible for the play at first; if the first play is at third, move toward the cutout. In either case, establish your set position before the play occurs.

4. *Timing!* Do not rule a runner out unless the fielder has complete control of the ball.

5. When the play is over, if a runner remains on base, observe the runner whenever the ball is near his location.

Plate umpire

1. Pause, read and react. Read ground ball and R3; determine where the first play will occur.

2. Clear the catcher; if the ball is hit near either foul line, straddle the line and observe the play. You must first rule fair or foul without hindering R3's advance toward home plate.

3. If fair/foul is not a concern: If R3 advances to score, prepare for a play at the plate by establishing your position 10-12 feet from the plate and your 90-degree angle between your line of sight and the throw. Be certain neither the catcher's nor the runner's body will block your view of the potential tag. If the first play is at first base, observe the play and be prepared to rule on interference by B1 or an overthrow; offer your opinion of a swipe tag or pulled foot only if U1 requests help.

5. You are responsible for any play that develops at home plate.

Notes

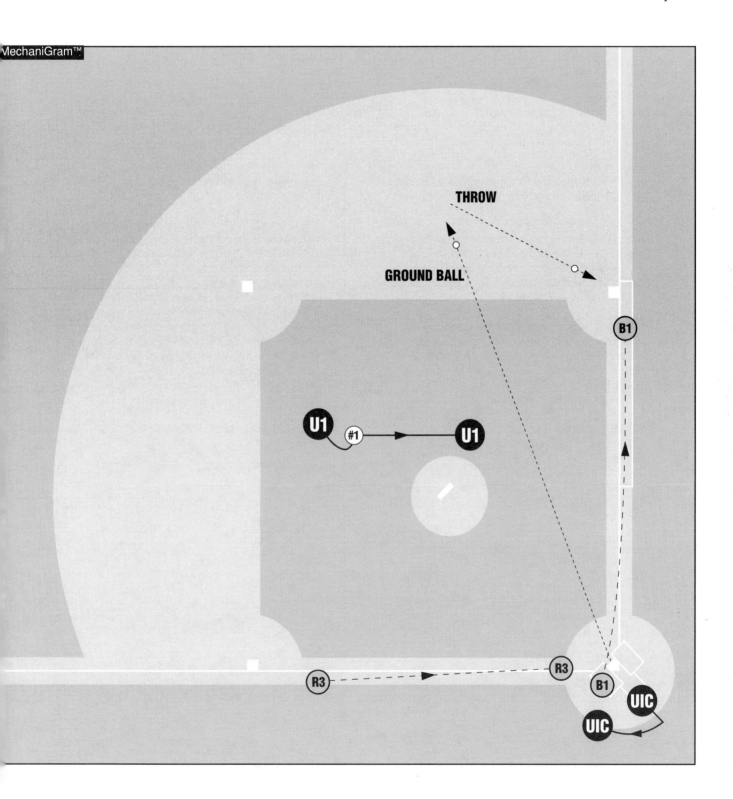

THROW

GROUND BALL

Case Study 59 — Bunt

Game situation: Runner at third

Action on the field: B1 bunts

RESPONSIBILITIES

Base umpire

1. Step up, turn and face the ball; pause, read and react. Read the bunted ball, usually in "the box."

2. Read whether the play will develop at first, third or home. If the play is at first or third, react by moving aggressively toward the play. You are responsible for the first play at first or third and for any subsequent play that develops at first, second or third.

3. If you have the play, move to establish a 90-degree angle to the throw. If the play is at the plate (it is), prepare for a subsequent play at first or second.

5. When the play is over, if a runner remains on base, observe the runner whenever the ball is near his location.

Plate umpire

1. Pause, read and react. Read the bunted ball, usually in "the box."

2. Clear the catcher; rule fair or foul as necessary without hindering R3's advance to the plate.

3. If fair/foul is not a concern: If R3 advances to score, prepare for a play at the plate by establishing your position 10-12 feet from the plate and your 90-degree angle between your line of sight and the throw. Be certain neither the catcher's nor the runner's body will block your view of the potential tag. If the first play is at first base, observe the play and be prepared to rule on interference by B1 or an overthrow; offer your opinion of a swipe tag or pulled foot only if U1 requests help.

4. You are responsible for any play that develops at home plate.

Notes

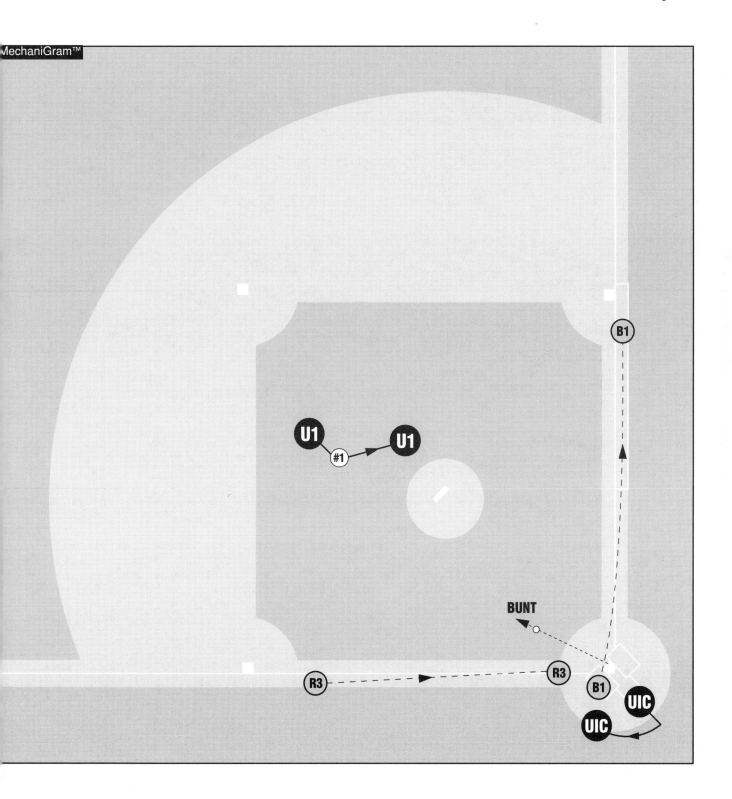

Review: Runner at third

Base umpire
- Start in position C.
- Fair/foul: You have no responsibility.
- Field coverage: You have the "V," beginning with any ball hit directly to F7 and ending with any ball hit directly to F9.
- On the bases: You have all plays at first, second and third base.
- Priorities:
    1. A balk or illegal pitch.
    2. Help for the plate umpire on the check-swing.
    3. Pick off attempt at third base by the pitcher or catcher.
    4. A "trouble ball" in your area of the outfield — the "V," beginning with any ball hit directly to F7 and ending with any ball hit directly to F9.
    5. A ground ball in the infield: You have all plays at first, second and third.
    6. A batted or bunted ball with F1, F3, F4 and/or B1 converging at the base.
    7. A ball hit to the outfield followed by a play on B1 at any base.

Umpire in chief
- Your first concern is always the pitch: strike or ball.
- Fair/foul: You have all fair/foul decisions.
- Field coverage: You have balls hit to the outfield to the left or right of the "V."
- On the bases: You have all plays at home plate.
- Priorities:
    1. A balk or illegal pitch.
    2. The pitch: ball or strike.
    3. Check-swings and defensive appeals.
    4. A fair/foul call down either foul line.
    5. A "trouble" ball in your area of the outfield.
    6. Any play at home plate.
    7. A bunted ball when opponents converge — interference/obstruction.

Quiz

Without referring back, you should be able to answer the following true-false questions. Remember: R1 is always the runner who begins a play at first base; R2 at second; R3 at third; B1 is the batter-runner; fielders are identified by their scoring abbreviations (F1 is the pitcher, F2 the catcher, etc.).

1. On a "trouble" ball in the "V," U1 will go to the outfield grass to rule catch/no catch because there is only one runner on base.
2. UIC always has R3's tag up after a caught batted ball.
3. U1 starts in position C. If the left fielder moves four to six steps toward the line and attempts a diving catch, U1 has the catch/no catch decision.
4. B1 hits a fair ball down the left-field line for extra bases. After R3 scores, UIC will move up and cover third base.
5. On a fly ball to straight-away center field, the best place for UIC to be to observe R3 tagging up is straddling the mid-point of the third-base line.
6. If R3 attempts to steal home, UIC must call the pitch first, then determine whether R3 is out or safe.

Runner configuration: Runners at second and third

Base umpire position: Position C.

   Adjustment factors: (New umpires should work in the basic position. If you have at least three years of field experience, consider the following points and determine whether you want to adjust from your basic position.)

   Game situation: If the infield is playing "in," adjust your position left or right to allow the second baseman plenty of room to field a batted ball.

   Defensive tendencies: A pickoff throw to *either* second or third by the pitcher should result in an excellent look from position B, particularly if you work deep. Do not hesitate to work at the edge of the infield grass.

   In order of importance, be prepared for the following situations:
   1. A balk or illegal pitch.
   2. Help for the plate umpire on the check-swing.
   3. Pick off attempt at third base by the pitcher.
   4. Pick off attempt at third base by the catcher.
   5. Pick off attempt at second base by the pitcher.
   6. A "trouble" ball in your area of the outfield — the "V," beginning with any ball hit directly to F7 and ending with any ball hit directly to F9.
   7. A ground ball in the infield: You have all plays at first, second and third. UIC has responsibility for any play that develops at home plate.
   8. A batted or bunted ball with F1, F3, F4 and/or B1 converging at the base.
   9. A ball hit to the outfield followed by any play at first, second or third.

Plate umpire anticipation:

Your initial position is always behind the plate. As the pitcher begins his delivery, come set in your stance. Your initial responsibility is always calling the pitch a strike or a ball. Respond to the batted ball and the action as it develops.

   Batted ball in the infield: Determine fair/foul as appropriate. U1 will rule on all plays at first, second and third; you have complete responsibility for any play at home plate. Cover dead-ball areas in case of an errant throw.

   Batted ball to the outfield: You have the areas from F7 to the left-field dead-ball area and from F9 to the right-field dead-ball area. *Stay home!* You must see R3 tagging up and any play at the plate. To right field: Take a position a few feet up the first-base line; rule fair/foul and catch/no catch as necessary. To left field: Take a position a few feet up the third-base line; rule fair/foul, catch/no catch as necessary.

   In order of importance, be prepared for the following situations:
   1. A balk or illegal pitch.
   2. The pitch: ball or strike.
   3. Check-swings and defensive appeals.
   4. A fair/foul call down either foul line.
   5. A tag play on R3 trying to score.
   6. A "trouble" ball in your area of the outfield.
   7. A subsequent play on R2 at home plate.
   8. A bunted ball when opponents converge — interference/obstruction.

Case Study 60 — Stealing home!

Game situation: Runners at second and third

Action on the field: R3 is stealing the plate

RESPONSIBILITIES

Base umpire	Plate umpire
1. Read the runner's break in your peripheral vision.	1. Concentrate.
2. Remain alert for a batted ball.	2. Determine whether the pitch is a ball or strike.
3. If the ball clears the batter, read R2. If he advances, move cautiously toward the midpoint of the third-base line. There may be a subsequent play on R2, either at third if he advances or at second if he starts toward third and retreats.	3. Do not attempt to remove your mask; step forward as the catcher moves to apply the tag; observe the action as best you can.
	4. *First* call the pitch; *second* declare R3 safe or out.
	5. If the pitch gets past the catcher, prepare for a subsequent tag play at the plate — R2 may attempt to score on the wild pitch.

Notes

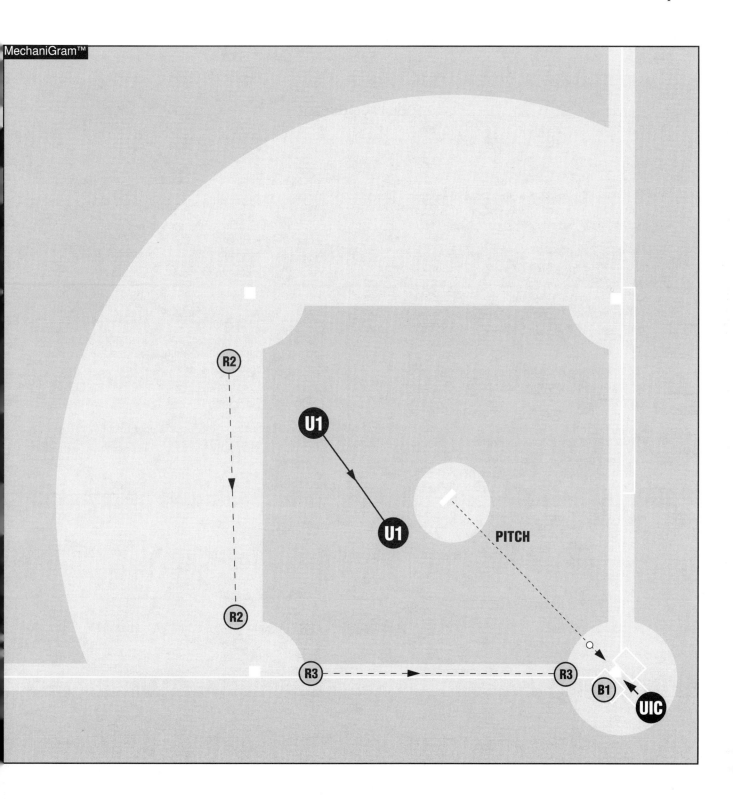

Case Study 61 — Fly ball in the "V"

Game situation: Runners at second and third

Action on the field: B1 flies to the middle of the outfield

RESPONSIBILITIES

Base umpire	Plate umpire

Base umpire

1. Step up, turn and face the ball; pause, read and react. Read the position of the fielder making the play and determine whether this is a ball in your coverage area (it is) and whether this is a "trouble" ball.

2. If you read a "trouble" ball, move toward the coming play, but only to the edge of the infield grass. *Do not leave the infield grass!* If it is not a "trouble" ball, move two or three steps back toward the pitcher's mound to "open" your field of view. You must see the catch in the outfield as you observe R2 tagging up and B1 touching first base.

3. If there is a catch (there is), signal only if the catch is made "below the knee"; verbally inform your partner of a routine catch. If a difficult play results in no catch, signal "safe" and verbally call, "No catch! No catch!"

4. After the catch: You are responsible for a play at second or third base on R2. If there is no catch, you are responsible for any play that develops at first, second or third. Establish your set position before the play occurs. *Timing!*

5. If a runner remains on base, observe the runner whenever the ball is near his location.

Plate umpire

1. Pause, read and react. Read the developing play and your partner.

2. With the ball in U1's coverage area, move toward the third-base dugout to observe the play. This will open your angle and let you observe the fielder's catch and R3 tagging up.

4. After the catch: You have responsibility for any play that develops on R3 at home plate. If R3 tries to score, return to home plate and read the throw. If a play develops at the plate, establish your set position before the play occurs. *Timing!*

5. Remain alert. A subsequent play could develop with R2 attempting to score.

Notes

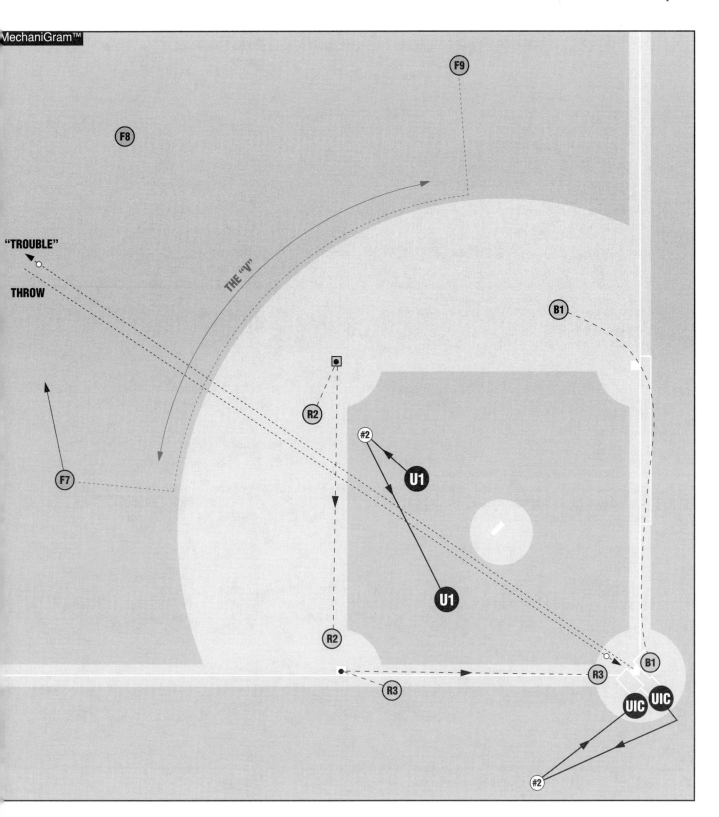

Case Study 62 — Fly ball to left field

Game situation: Runners at second and third base

Action on the field: Left fielder moves toward the line on a fly ball

RESPONSIBILITIES

Base umpire	Plate umpire
1. Step up, turn and face the ball; pause, read and react. Read the position of the fielder making the play and determine whether this is a ball in your coverage area (it is not).	1. Pause, read and react. Read the position of the fielder making the play and determine whether this is a ball in your coverage area (it is) and whether this is a "trouble" ball.
2. Since the ball is not in your area: Move two or three steps back toward the pitcher's mound to "open" your field of view. Remain aware of the fly ball status as you observe R2 tagging up and B1 touching first base. Listen for your partner to inform you of a catch.	2. Since the ball is in your coverage area, clear the catcher and communicate with your partner: "I'm on the line!" If fair/foul is a consideration or if it is a "trouble" ball, you'll have to establish a position near the third-base line with an unobstructed view of the fielder making the play, but *stay near home!* If fair/foul is not a consideration and it is not a "trouble" ball, move toward the third-base dugout to observe the play. This will open your angle and let you observe the fielder's catch and R3 tagging up. You are responsible for any play that develops at home plate.
	3. Develop the best angle possible to observe the catch/no catch.
5. After the catch: You are responsible for a play at second or third base on R2. If there is no catch, you are responsible for any play that develops at first, second or third. Establish your set position before the play occurs. *Timing!*	4. If there is a catch (there is), signal only if the catch is made "below the knee"; verbally inform your partner of any catch: "Bill, that's a catch." If the ball is a hit, you are responsible for any play that develops at home plate.
	5. After the catch: You have responsibility for R3 tagging up. If R3 tries to score, return to home plate and read the throw. If a play develops at the plate, establish your set position before the play occurs. *Timing!*
7. If a runner remains on base, observe the runner whenever the ball is near his location.	6. Remain alert. A subsequent play could develop with R2 attempting to score.

Notes

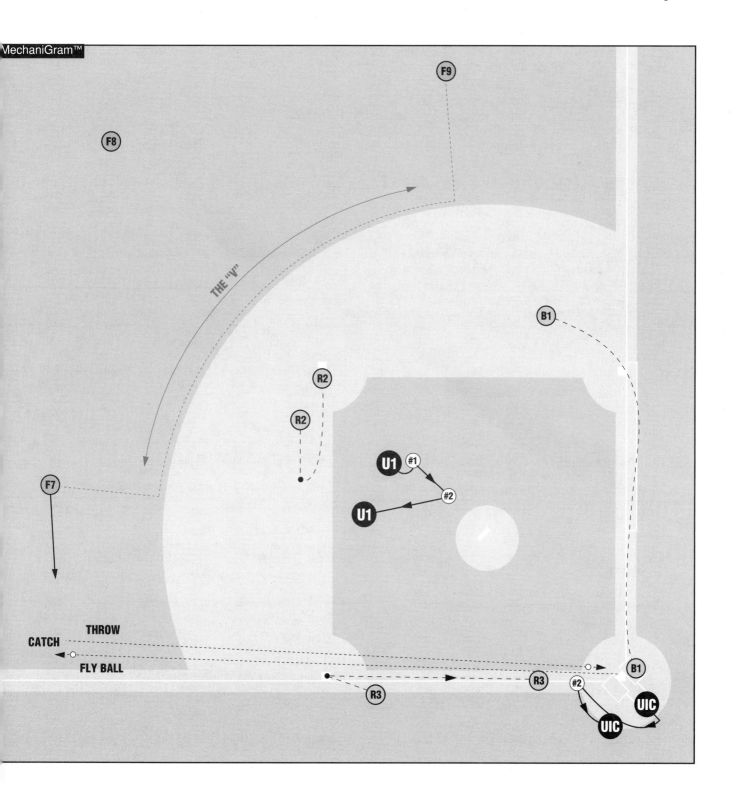

Case Study 63 — Fly ball to right field

Game situation: Runners at second and third base

Action on the field: Right fielder moves toward the line on a fly ball

RESPONSIBILITIES

Base umpire	Plate umpire
1. Step up, turn and face the ball; pause, read and react. Read the position of the fielder making the play and determine whether this is a ball in your coverage area (it is not).	1. Pause, read and react. Read the position of the fielder making the play and determine whether this is a ball in your coverage area (it is) and whether this is a "trouble" ball.
2. Since the ball is not in your area: Move two or three steps toward position C and back toward the pitcher's mound to "open" your field of view. Remain aware of the fly ball status as you observe R2 tagging up and B1 touching first base. Listen for your partner to inform you of a catch.	2. Since the ball is in your coverage area, clear the catcher and communicate with your partner: "I'm on the line!" If fair/foul is a consideration or if it is a "trouble" ball, move a short distance up the first-base line to observe the play. You must remain close enough to home plate to return in time to be in position for a play at the plate if R3 tags up or tries to score. Your first priority is the batted ball; after you determine fair/foul and catch/no catch, take a quick glance toward the runner tagging up at third base. It is a difficult look. Remember: Your first priority is the ball! If fair/foul is not a consideration and it is not a "trouble" ball, move toward the third-base dugout to observe the play. This will open your angle and let you observe the fielder's catch and R3 tagging up. You are responsible for any play that develops at home plate.
5. After the catch: You are responsible for a play at second or third base on R2. If there is no catch, you are responsible for any play that develops at first, second or third. Establish your set position before the play occurs. *Timing!*	3. Develop the best angle possible to observe the catch/no catch.
	4. If there is a catch (there is), signal only if the catch is made "below the knee"; verbally inform your partner of any catch: "Bill, that's a catch." If the ball is a hit, you are responsible for any play that develops at home plate.
7. If a runner remains on base, observe the runner whenever the ball is near his location.	5. After the catch: You have responsibility for R3 tagging up. If R3 tries to score, return to home plate and read the throw. If a play develops at the plate, establish your set position before the play occurs. *Timing!*
	6. Remain alert. A subsequent play could develop with R2 attempting to score.

Notes

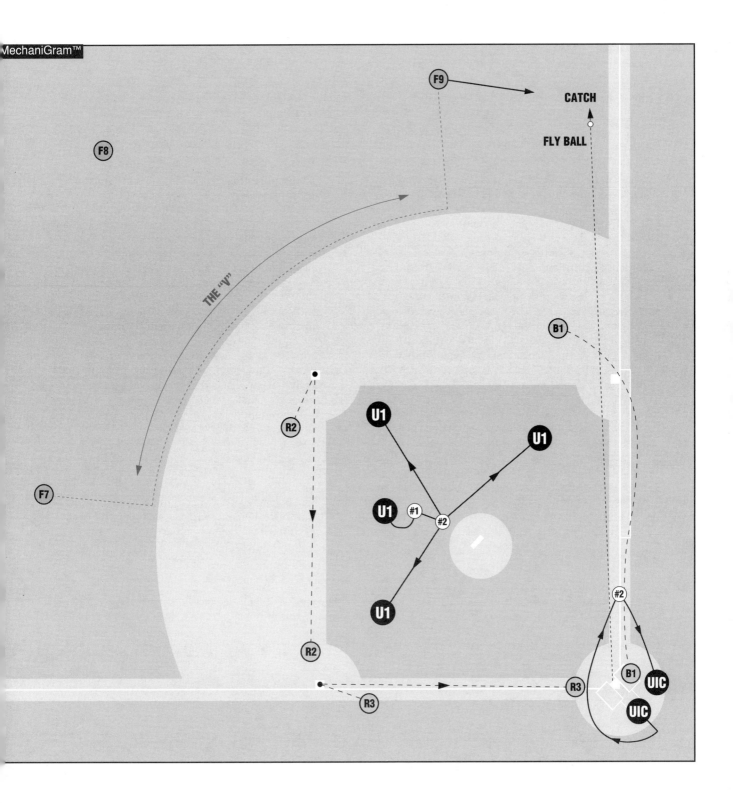

Case Study 64 — Ground ball to the infield

Game situation: Runners at second and third

Action on the field: B1 hits ground ball played in the infield

RESPONSIBILITIES

Base umpire	Plate umpire
1. Step up, turn and face the ball. Read ground ball and determine where the first play will occur.	1. Pause, read and react. Read ground ball and R3; determine where the first play will occur.
2. Realize a first play at second or third is possible, and that in most cases the infielder will "look" the runners back, then throw to first. You are responsible for any play that occurs at first, second or third base.	2. Clear the catcher; if the ball is hit near either foul line, straddle the line and observe the play. You must first rule fair or foul without hindering R3's advance toward home plate.
3. Keep your chest to the ball. Let the infielder's throw turn you to the play. If the first play develops at first base, move several steps across the infield behind the mound, move toward the first base line if there is time, and establish the best angle possible for the play at first; if the first play is at second or third, move toward the cutout at that base. Establish your set position before the play occurs.	3. If fair/foul is not a concern: If R3 advances to score, prepare for a play at the plate by establishing your position 10 to 12 feet from the plate and a 90-degree angle between your line of sight and the throw. Be certain neither the catcher's nor the runner's body will block your view of the potential tag. If the first play is at first base, observe the play and be prepared to rule on interference by B1 or an overthrow; offer your opinion of a swipe tag or pulled foot only if U1 requests help.
4. *Timing!* Do not rule a runner out unless the fielder has complete control of the ball.	
5. When the play is over, if a runner remains on base, observe the runner whenever the ball is near his location.	5. You are responsible for any play that develops at home plate. Remain alert; a subsequent play could develop with R2 attempting to score.

Notes

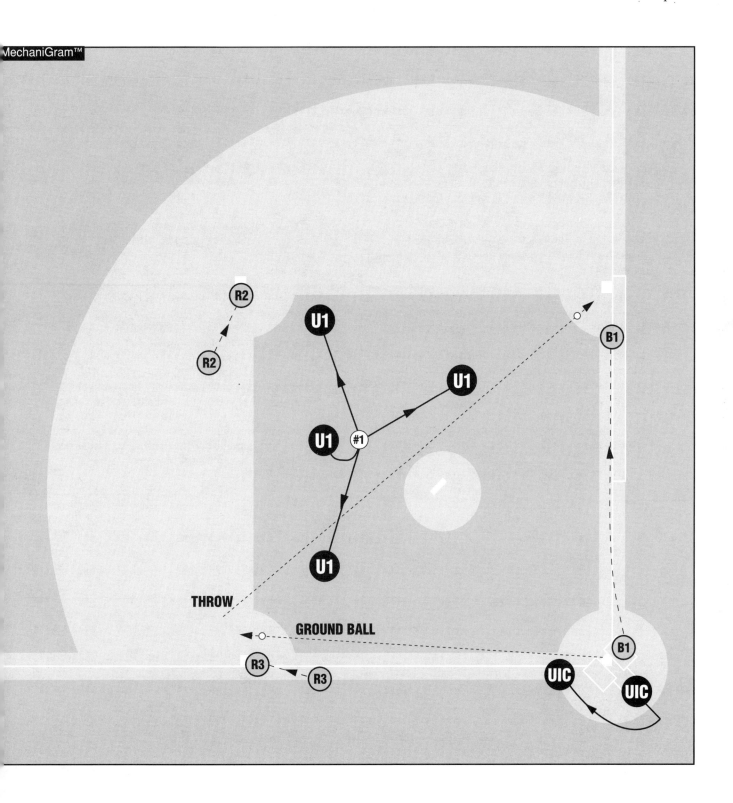

Case Study 65 — Bunt

Game situation: Runners at second and third

Action on the field: B1 bunts

RESPONSIBILITIES

Base umpire	Plate umpire
1. Step up, turn and face the ball; pause, read and react. Read the bunted ball, usually in "the box."	1. Pause, read and react. Read the bunted ball, usually in "the box."
2. If the first play is at first, second or third, react by moving aggressively toward the play. You are responsible for any play that develops at first, second or third.	2. Clear the catcher; rule fair or foul as necessary without hindering R3's advance to the plate.
3. If you have the play, move to establish a 90-degree angle to the throw. If the play is at the plate (it is), prepare for a subsequent play at first, second or third.	3. If fair/foul is not a concern: If R3 advances to score, prepare for a play at the plate by establishing your position 10 to 12 feet from the plate and a 90-degree angle between your line of sight and the throw. Be certain neither the catcher's nor the runner's body will block your view of the potential tag. If the first play is at first base, observe the play and be prepared to rule on interference by B1 or an overthrow; offer your opinion of a swipe tag or pulled foot only if U1 requests help.
5. When the play is over, if a runner remains on base, observe the runner whenever the ball is near his location.	4. You are responsible for any play that develops at home plate. Remain alert; a subsequent play could develop with R2 attempting to score.

Notes

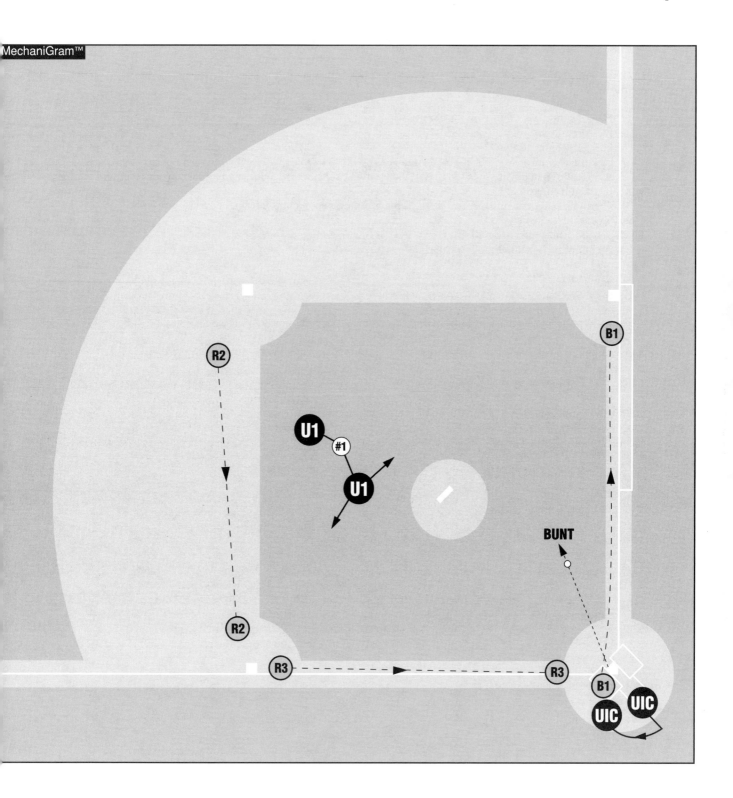

Review: Runners at second and third

Base umpire
- Start in position C.
- Adjust based on the game situation and defensive tendencies.
- Fair/foul: You have no responsibility.
- Field coverage: You have the "V," beginning with any ball hit directly to F7 and ending with any ball hit directly to F9.
- On the bases: You have all plays at first, second and third base.
- Priorities:
    1. A balk or illegal pitch.
    2. Help for the plate umpire on the check-swing.
    3. Pick off attempt at third base by the pitcher.
    4. Pick off attempt at third base by the catcher.
    5. Pick off attempt at second base by the pitcher.
    6. A "trouble" ball in your area of the outfield — the "V," beginning with any ball hit directly to F7 and ending with any ball hit directly to F9.
    7. A ground ball in the infield: You have all plays at first, second and third. UIC has responsibility for any play that develops at home plate.
    8. A batted or bunted ball with F1, F3, F4 and/or B1 converging at the base.
    9. A ball hit to the outfield followed by any play at first, second or third.

Umpire in chief
- Your first concern is always the pitch: strike or ball.
- Fair/foul: You have all fair/foul decisions.
- Field coverage: You have balls hit to the outfield to the left or right of the "V."
- On the bases: Stay home; you have all plays at home plate.
- Priorities:
    1. A balk or illegal pitch.
    2. The pitch: ball or strike.
    3. Check-swings and defensive appeals.
    4. A fair/foul call down either foul line.
    5. A tag play on R3 trying to score.
    6. A "trouble" ball in your area of the outfield.
    7. A subsequent play on R2 at home plate.
    8. A bunted ball when opponents converge — interference/obstruction.

Quiz

Without referring back, you should be able to answer the following true-false questions. Remember: R1 is always the runner who begins a play at first base; R2 at second; R3 at third; B1 is the batter-runner; fielders are identified by their scoring abbreviations (F1 is the pitcher, F2 the catcher, etc.).

1. When the left fielder runs straight in and attempts a diving catch, UIC determines catch/no catch.

2. When the center fielder runs straight in and attempts a diving catch, U1 determines catch/no catch.

3. When the right fielder runs straight in and attempts a diving catch, U1 determines catch/no catch.

4. On a ground ball to the first baseman, U1 should move directly toward the first-base cutout.

5. On a "trouble" ball in the "V," U1 must remain on the infield grass to determine catch/no catch.

6. On a "trouble" ball in the "V," U1 must determine catch/no catch, then cover the play at third if R2 attempts to advance.

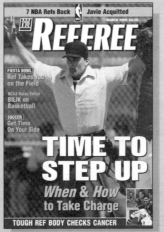
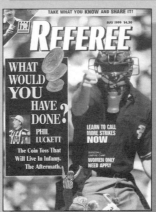

If you like this book, check out the complete Baseball Umpires Guidebooks collection and these other informative, info-packed publications on baseball umpiring from *Referee* Books and the National Association of Sports Officials!

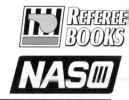

Each volume is presented in an easy-to-read, 8 ½" x 11" workbook format with detailed graphics, explanations, section reviews and quizzes.

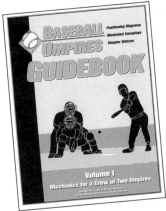

Volume I, Proper Positioning

The most comprehensive book on umpire positioning available anywhere. Complete with positioning diagrams, end-of-chapter quizzes, and caseplays covering proper positioning for every situation! Information is presented in a clear, easy-to-read workbook format. You'll learn where to be, when and (most important) *why!*

Includes: Where to start each play • Where to go when the ball is hit • What to watch for and why • The latest two-man innovations • Helpful tips to make difficult coverage easier • Complete explanations why each position recommended is better than its alternatives • A solid review of each umpire's positioning responsibilities and priorities • More than 60 case situations with complete breakdowns for both umpires • Case studies, reviews and quiz materials to help you measure comprehension. (paperback, 166 pages)

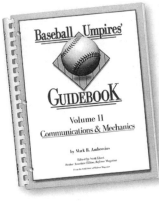

Volume II, Communications and Mechanics

Presents step-by-step information about **where** you are supposed to go during a play, **what** you have to do to insure you effectively cover the action working in a two-man crew, and **why** many of the seemingly "little" things are so important.

Includes: Communication and mechanics keys with the latest two-man innovations • Helpful tips to make difficult situations easier • Complete explanations of why recommended coverage is better than the alternatives • A solid review of each umpire's communication and mechanics responsibilities • More than 60 case situations with complete breakdowns for both umpires, including run-downs. (paperback, 169 pages)

Volume III, Three-man & Four-man Mechanics

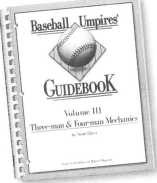

Whether you work a full schedule of college three-man games or you're preparing for an end-of-the-season tournament that will use four-man crews, this is the reference book that provides the information you'll need to get ready.

Includes: A basic discussion of the different responsibilities assigned to each umpire on three-man and four-man crews • A review of basic on-field rotations — where to go, when, why, and what to look for • A conversational approach to trouble areas — plays that do happen, and do present coverage problems for three-man and four-man crews • Clean, concise, three-man and four-man pregame outlines to help lead the discussion and coordinate the crew's efforts • Case studies • Plays and coverages with a step-by-step explanation of what each umpire does — complete with full-field diagrams — for dozens of play scenarios. (paperback, 211 pages)

Guidebook List Price:	$32.95 each
Referee Price:	$29.95 You Save $3!
NASO-Member Price:	$23.95 You Save $9!

Set of Three + Binder: $79.95
($63.95 for NASO members)

Binder only: $7.95
($6.35 for NASO members)

Bulk order discounts available!

Smart Baseball Umpiring — How to Get Better Every Game

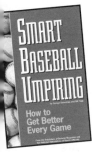

Anyone who has umpired a while knows outs and safes, balls and strikes are *not* what umpiring is all about. Your presentation and mental approach are equally important when defining the complete umpire. Veteran umpire George Demetriou and *Referee* editor Bill Topp explore various ways to get ready and improve every game. Included: The mobile plate umpire • Analyzing your performance • 30 ways to balk • Admitting mistakes • Rise above it all — This chapter helps you get back to basics — mentally. Great information for rookies and veterans alike! (9" x 6" paperback, 84 pages) **BSBU, $12.95, NASO-Member Price: $10.35**

19 Smart Moves For The Baseball Umpire

Includes tips on handling pregame meetings, ejections, forfeits, incident reports, arguments and more! Written by Ken Allan, veteran NCAA Division I baseball umpire. (24-page booklet)
BSMBA, $2.95, NASO-Member Price: $2.35

All Sports
All Levels
Always
There For You

The National Association of Sports Officials

- NASO's "Members Only Edition" of *Referee* magazine every month. Members receive 96-pages of *Referee* with 16-pages of association news, "members only" tips; case plays and educational product discounts.

- Members receive a *FREE* educational publication valued up to $9.95.

- Discounts on NASO/*Referee* publications such as the Officials' Guidebooks, rules comparisons and sport-specific preseason publications make you a better official.

- Referral service in the event you move to another community.

- Web page and e-mail communications keep you updated on NASO news, services and benefits.

- "Ask Us" rules interpretations service.

- Sports-specific rules quizzes.

- Free NASO e-mail address.

- Free access to the *NASO LockerRoom* — an NASO cyberspace service.

- Membership Certificate and laminated membership card.

- NASO Code of Ethics.

For a complete brochure and membership information contact:
NASO • 2017 Lathrop Avenue • Racine, WI 53405 • 262/632-5448 • 262/632-5460 (fax)
naso@naso.org or visit our website at www.naso.org